THE PROMISE OF GOD'S PRESENCE

One Man's Journey Through Cancer

CHRIS BINGAMAN
AS TOLD TO DON HAWKINS

BACK TO THE BIBLE ®
Lincoln, Nebraska

12,000 printed to date— 1997
(1170-031— 12M— 497)
ISBN 0-8474-1713-1

Unless otherwise noted, all Scripture is taken from the
New International Version, © 1973, 1978, 1984 by the
International Bible Society.

Printed in the United States of America.

About the Authors

Chris Bingaman is a partner with his father, Max, in Bingaman and Son Lumber Company. He and his wife, Heidi, live near Kreamer, Pennsylvania, with their four daughters, Emily, Lindsey, Leah and Audrey. The Bingamans attend Winfield Baptist Church, in Winfield, Pennsylvania, where Chris teaches an adult Sunday school class. After his two-year ordeal with multiple myeloma, Chris has been free of symptoms for four years.

Don Hawkins is cohost and producer of the *Back to the Bible* radio program, which is heard on more than 600 stations worldwide. He has authored or coauthored many best-selling books, including *Never Give Up, How to Beat Burnout, When Cancer Comes, Prodigal People, Master Discipleship, Overworked* and *The Roots of Inner Peace.*

Don is a veteran conference and seminar speaker and has 19 years of pastoral experience. He and his wife, Kathy, are the parents of three grown children and live in Lincoln, Nebraska.

Acknowledgments

It is difficult to give proper recognition to everyone who contributes to a project like this. We especially want to thank Chris's wife, Heidi, his parents, Max and Martha Bingaman, as well as Chris's sisters: Tammy, Lori, Heidi and Mary Beth.

We are especially grateful to Dr. Woodrow Kroll, President of Back to the Bible, whose vision and encouragement helped bring this book to pass, and to Art Figurski, who initiated the contact between the Bingaman family and Dr. Kroll. Many people, including Dave Dravecky, provided significant encouragement both before and during the project.

Once the writing process was underway, we used the editorial expertise of Rachel Derowitsch and Allen Bean and the typing skills of Susan Hertzler with assistance from Dawn Leuschen, Nancy Breese and Janet Miller. Layout and production were coordinated by Blaine Smith and Kirk Greuter.

Above all, we are grateful to the Lord God, whose love and presence made this story possible.

Chris Bingaman
Don Hawkins

Spring 1997

Foreword

Some time ago, a friend of mine asked me to telephone and encourage a friend of his. The friend he wanted me to call was Chris Bingaman, who had just been diagnosed with multiple myeloma. You see, several years ago God entrusted to me and my wife, Jan, a ministry to encourage cancer patients and amputees. I am a cancer survivor as well as an amputee; I lost my left arm due to cancer.

Even after going through this myself and understanding to some degree what people experience when hearing the word *cancer* for the first time, it doesn't make encouraging cancer patients and amputees any easier. And this call to Chris was no different. I was scared, as I am most of the time when making these calls, and I really didn't know what I would say to him. But I prayed and asked God to help me as I began to dial his number at the hospital. What made it even more difficult was that he was in the middle of treatments and I didn't know how he was going to feel.

When he picked up the phone and I heard his voice, it felt like my heart was in my throat. As we began to talk with each other, however, I became more and more comfortable. Before long, I realized that Chris Bingaman was encouraging me.

I learned something that day— never be afraid to call and express your feelings. Even to a stranger who is hurting, it is uplifting to know that there is someone out there who cares about what he is going through. You never know what surprises God may have in store as you step out of your comfort zone and do something that you know pleases Him. In this case, the encourager was being encouraged!

In my book *The Worth of a Man*, I related an account from Chris's experience that tells what kind of man he is and what kind of family he has. You'll find Chris's description of this incident in chapter 14 of *The Promise of His Presence*.

The weekend before he was diagnosed with multiple myeloma, Chris succumbed to back pain that left him lying on the floor of his family room, unable to move because of his intense suffering. The story relates how his dad comes in and finds Chris in that position. Wrapping his arms around his son and weeping, Chris's father cries out, "Oh, God, give me his pain."

The obvious love of this father for his son provides a beautiful picture of a Heavenly Father who loved His Son, yet allowed Him to suffer for us. I thank God for the testimony of the Bingaman family and their love for the Lord.

As you embark on this journey with the Bingamans, I pray God's presence through their story will encourage you as much as it has encouraged me.

Dave Dravecky

President,
Dave Dravecky's
Outreach of Hope

Contents

Introduction

Steel-gray clouds spattered intermittent rain as I turned my borrowed minivan north from Harrisburg, steering along the west bank of the Susquehanna River in central Pennsylvania. I was en route to meet Chris Bingaman and visit with his family about his experience with multiple myeloma, a rare form of cancer that attacks the bone marrow and is often fatal.

The weather seemed to provide an appropriately grim backdrop for the subject of cancer. This dreaded disease affects one individual in four and one family in three. Even though extensive research and new treatments have saved many lives, a high percentage of those diagnosed with cancer still consider it a death sentence. The options of surgery, radiation or chemotherapy, plus related side effects such as nausea and hair loss, permeate their lives with fear.

Several months earlier I had met Max and Martha Bingaman, Chris's parents, when they visited Back to the Bible's International Headquarters in Lincoln, Nebraska. During the renovation of our new headquarters building, Max had donated a trailer truck load of beautiful red oak lumber to be used for trim and door frames throughout our facility. In the words of our president, Woodrow Kroll, "The red oak lumber donated by Bingaman and Son sin-gle-handedly elevated the appearance of our new project from a standard, vanilla renovation to a beautiful finished product, far beyond what we could ever have afforded." The Bingamans had come to Lincoln to view the end result and to become better acquainted with our ministry team.

However, Dr. Kroll had already alerted me to the fact that there was more to the Bingaman story than just lumber. "Talk to Max and Martha about their son, Chris," he suggested with a smile. "I think you'll find at least an interview or two for our broadcast. In fact, there may even be a book in Chris's story."

As we stood talking in a narrow hallway on the second floor of the old Back to the Bible building in downtown Lincoln, I learned from Max and Martha how Chris had developed multiple myeloma, the same cancer that had killed Sam Walton, founder of the Wal-Mart chain of stores. Dr. Kroll was right— there was a story here. After telephone conversations with the Bingamans and further consultation with Dr. Kroll, I made plans to use some of the time I was scheduled to be in Pennsylvania for a speaking engagement to find out more about Chris and his heroic struggle against a killer disease.

* * *

The clouds began to break up a bit as I drove across an old, iron bridge into the small community of Kreamer, Pennsylvania. Following the detailed directions Chris had faxed me earlier, I made two left turns, then drove alongside a railroad spur until I spotted the sign that read "Bingaman and Son Lumber."

Inside, after a few minutes wait, I was greeted warmly by a sandy-haired, hazel-eyed young man with a fun-loving smile. A dusting of freckles covered his face. He was dressed in a casual sports shirt and tan slacks, and greeted me with a firm handshake. It didn't take me long to determine that Chris Bingaman still had a strong zest for life. When I asked him about his height, he admitted, "I was six foot one before I was diagnosed with cancer; now I'm just six foot. I shrank a bit." I suspected that his attitude had played an important role in his successful battle with cancer.

"I've been so excited to see how God has used the story of my cancer to encourage others," Chris acknowledged. "If Back to the Bible can help spread this story to even more people, I'll be grateful. That's all I'd like to see happen. I know firsthand how much suffering cancer can cause, and if God can use my cancer to point others to the Lord Jesus, that's what I want to see."

Less than an hour later, Chris and his wife, Heidi, plus Max and Martha joined me in the Elk Room, a spacious den that had been added to the back of the senior Bingaman's home. Large windows gave the room a feel of the outdoors, and the floor was made of the same red oak given to Back to the Bible. The walls were covered with ash and walnut paneling, and the vaulted ceiling was supported by ash beams—"We glue them here in our lumberyards," Max pointed out.

What impressed me most during this and subsequent visits with Chris and Heidi, Max and Martha, and the rest of the Bingamans was how they had recognized and drawn support from God's presence during this trying ordeal. When I was a pastor, I talked with many people who suffered through tragedies of various kinds. One typical response I've seen is "Why me?" Another is the angry complaint, "God is not fair. I didn't deserve this." There are many other variations on these common reactive themes as well.

As I talked with Chris and other members of his family at length, however, I saw a different attitude. Chris expressed it to me the first time we met. "Don, my question has been 'Why not me?' As a family, we often discussed how blessed we have been to be free of illness or tragedy. However, we were aware, and openly discussed, the possibility that things wouldn't always be that way. Sooner or later, one of us wouldn't be present for those special family gatherings. I'm convinced those honest discussions about our blessings and the unpredictability of the future helped prepare me for the time when I found out I had cancer."

I believe that the obvious gratitude Chris feels toward the Lord for His blessings, plus the recognition that, in a fallen world, no one is exempt from suffering, helped keep him aware of the promise of the Savior's presence. It hasn't been an easy journey. Yet in a real sense, as you read the story of Chris Bingaman, you'll be looking into the life of a man who has lived Psalm 23:4.

Yea, though I walk through the valley of the shadow of death, I will fear no evil; for You are with me; Your rod and Your staff, they comfort me.

During the two-year ordeal of his fight with multiple myeloma, Chris clearly saw the reality of the valley. As he told me following our meeting, "Don, this project has really made me think a lot about those years walking in the valley of death." Like King David, Chris looked death in the eye. He had been close enough to feel its icy grip. Others have experienced the same diagnosis as his and didn't live to tell about it. I'm confident you'll sense the courage Chris learned and used as he stood face-to-face with death and refused to blink.

A second thing that came through in my conversations with Chris and his family was their witness to the tenacity of the Lord's presence. Although Chris went through periods of struggle and doubt, he affirmed over and over how "God turned up my spiritual sensitivity to His presence in each of these situations." Like the psalmist, Chris came to say, "I will fear no evil, for You are with me."

Most of us have heard the story, oft repeated, of the man who complained to the Lord because during the darkest hours of his life, as he walked the sandy seashore, there was only one set of footsteps. "Lord, why were You not with me?" the man asked bitterly.

"You misunderstand, My child," the Lord is said to have replied. "During those darkest hours when you felt unable to go on, I carried you. Those footsteps were not yours, but Mine!" Unlike the young man in the "Footsteps" parable, Chris Bingaman refused to lose sight of the tenacious presence of a Savior who fulfilled His promise to be right there with him every step of the way.

Finally, talking with Chris and his family underscored the variety of God's encouragements to His suffering child. Time and time again the Bingamans were reminded by circumstances that God was still in control, and there was hope. As Chris told me, "I so vividly remember at times being as low emotionally as I've ever been in my life. Every time I would sink so low, I didn't know if I could go on. But God would send something or someone to give me a ray of hope. I shall never forget those times and how significant they've become to me."

It is our prayer as you read *The Promise of God's Presence* and learn the details of Chris Bingaman's journey through cancer, that whatever your circumstances, you will clearly see the tenacity of the Lord's presence and the variety of His specific encouragements to you, and that you will press on without losing hope.

Don Hawkins

Chapter 1

Trip of a Lifetime

Whenever I tell my story, I always begin in November 1991. It's as though the picture has been etched in vivid Technicolor in my mind's eye. I was sitting on a horse, surrounded by the beautiful mountains of Montana, with tears flowing from my eyes like water running off a snow melt.

Now these weren't tears of sorrow or grief. They were tears of joy, tears of gratitude. I remember the incredible feeling in my heart as I thought, *Lord, I can't begin to number all the things You have blessed me with. You've promised to be with me and You've been present with me all the way.*

There I was, 34 years old. I had a beautiful wife, four wonderful daughters, a new home, and as the son in Bingaman and Son Lumber Company, I had the best job any man could ever have.

My dad and I have been close for a long time. People tell us we look alike. I have his same quick grin, his sense of humor, his love for people, and even his industrial-sized smile.

We sure had a lot to smile about on this trip. We were doing something we both loved a great deal—hunting elk. It was the trip of a lifetime, and I remember being elated as we walked through the Northwest terminal in the Minneapolis airport, hurrying to catch our connecting flight to Montana. I started thinking, *Man, how lucky could a guy be.* Then as we flew into Montana and I saw those beautiful, snow-covered mountains, I thought, *It's more than luck; it's God's blessing. He's been so kind to me.*

Dad had picked out a beautiful facility, the Lost Fork Ranch. We had a duplex, a log cabin nestled in the mountains near the Lee Metcalf National Forest. It couldn't have been any more picturesque. The Madison River flowed just below our cabin, and we were virtually surrounded by mountains. In fact, it was so rugged we had to ride into the hunting area and out on horseback.

Each day while Dad and I rode out to hunt elk, Mom and Heidi, my wife, were able to watch the action through a telescope they had mounted near the lodge. They could see us actually chasing the elk. In fact, I think Heidi was looking at me when I shot my elk, but she wasn't as excited about it as I was.

I had been involved in hunting of one kind or another ever since I was old enough to know which end of a gun meant business. My dream had always been to kill a bull elk. So I finally had shot my first one— a huge bull. When Dad bagged his elk, we both fulfilled a lifelong ambition.

After dinner the following evening, Heidi and I knocked on Mom and Dad's door. Heidi was carrying Audrey, our three-month old. We walked into Mom and Dad's sitting area, and we both just started crying.

Mom and Dad looked at us with typical parental concern and said, "What's wrong? Tell us what's the matter."

I'm not sure whether Heidi or I spoke first, but I remember what we told them. "There's nothing wrong. We just don't know how to express to the two of you how much we've appreciated the privilege of being brought out here and given an opportunity to see all this, and to enjoy this fantastic experience."

Life was wonderful. We had enjoyed this dream trip with my parents, and I had succeeded in my goal of shooting an elk. Then came that final day, a Saturday. The sun was setting as I rode down the mountain toward camp. I could hear coyotes howling, and the mountains were glowing with the light of the setting sun. In that sunset, I sensed the Lord's presence as He spoke to my heart about all the things He had blessed me with. I never felt better or more healthy in my life, or more grateful.

Little did I know that, in just a few short weeks, my life would change forever. I'd be walking through the valley of the shadow of death. There were plenty of times when I didn't think I'd make it. But before I go into detail about that, let me tell you about my family.

Chapter 2

The
Bingaman Clan

We've always been a close family. That's a trite saying, but it's certainly been true for us. Mom and Dad have four girls and me, plus 15 grandchildren— 3 grandsons and 12 granddaughters. I guess our family must be genetically predisposed to have more girls than guys.

Our family get-togethers resemble scenes from the old Walton family television show. The whole tribe gathers at Dad and Mom's every Sunday after church for dinner, and the meal typically resembles a Thanksgiving feast. The dining room table seats 18, plus there's a small table for four of the smaller grandchildren and another table that can accommodate six to eight older grandchildren in the Elk Room, a huge den enclosed in glass.

Dad always asks the blessing over these occasions, thanking the Lord for the food and the privilege for all of us to be together again. I used to take these family gatherings for granted, but my journey through cancer helped me realize the blessing of family closeness. I recall many of the Sundays when I was away in Arkansas for treatment when we would phone home and find the family— including our four daughters— gathered as usual. It was so encouraging to know our daughters were surrounded by family members who cared for them and loved them in our absence. We also sensed their prayers, love and concern for me while Heidi and I were away.

I've already indicated how wonderful I feel my parents are. Mom has large, brown eyes, and she's the most unselfish, giving person I've ever known. Mom just fits the Proverbs 31 godly woman like a hand in a glove. I also agree with her description of Dad— "Unbeatable as a husband and father, giving and compassionate." Dad always has been an ideal father.

My sister Tammy is the oldest, next to me. She's petite, with blonde hair and large brown eyes, like Mom's. Tammy and her husband, Tim Faust, have two sons, Nicholas and Benjamin, and a daughter, Ashley. Lori, my next sister, and her husband, Bill Ermert, have five daughters, Elizabeth, Rachel, Amanda, Melissa and Allison. Then there's Heidi and her husband, Dan Conklin. They have three children, Brooke, Cody and Bethany. My youngest sister is Mary Beth. You'll learn several special things about her as I tell this story.

Bingaman and Son Lumber is one of the two largest companies in Kreamer, Pennsylvania. My grandfather started the business right after the Depression in the early 1940s. He did a lot of business with the mines in eastern Pennsylvania. Kreamer is located about 40 miles from the heart of mining country. In the '40s the mining business began to die out, and Grandpa began selling what we call "grade lumber" to different furniture plants, a store fixture plant and a handle factory. By the time Dad graduated from high school, he wanted to go into business with Grandpa, but Grandpa had been through the Depression, and, being conservative, didn't believe the business could make ends meet with Dad on the payroll. So Dad began working at a factory in Kreamer.

After Dad had worked at the factory for about eight years and helped Grandpa during the evenings, the big break finally came. A customer in New Jersey promised Dad— who was good at selling— that he'd purchase a large quantity of lumber from us. Dad and Mom, who had been married only a short time, drove to New Jersey to see these people, and they promised to buy "all the lumber you can send us."

According to Dad, these people were in the picture frame business. He and Mom returned home elated because he really wanted to go into the lumber business with Grandpa. About three weeks after Dad had given the plant six weeks' notice that he was quitting, Grandpa received a written notice from the company in New Jersey to hold all shipments until October. Grandpa, who had been very concerned about adding Dad to the business anyway, drove over to the plant where Dad was working and urged him to go to his boss and tell him he had decided not to quit. Being a man of faith, Dad told Grandpa, "I believe the Lord is just testing us to see whether we are going to trust Him or not. Let's just trust the Lord and go ahead with this commitment."

The rest is history. Grandpa Bingaman never saw the business as it is today, because he died in 1969. His name was Carson, and he and Dad had a wonderful relationship, much like the close relationship Dad and I have.

I've always loved the lumber business. From the time I was three, I rode with Dad on the delivery truck. At that time Dad drove a truck daily, and I went along with him every chance I got. When I was old enough I started working in the lumberyard. When I graduated from Middleburg Joint High School, I received a partial scholarship to Messiah College, where I planned to play soccer. My goal, however, was to come back, join the company and work in the lumber business with Dad.

When I returned home after that first year, I marched into Dad's office and announced, "Dad, I'm not going back to school. Not one of the courses I have to take next year pertains to our business." As things worked out, Dad desperately needed someone to work right then. The company was growing, and he felt overwhelmed. So I quit college and came to work. I had a natural aptitude for selling and finally worked my way up, with Dad's encouragement, to become vice president of sales.

* * *

Dad and Mom met early— in fact, they knew each other when they were children. Their families attended church together in Middleburg. It was in that church that my dad first heard the Gospel preached by a man named Sidney Cox, a graduate of Moody Bible Institute. (I believe he is the man who wrote the song "My Lord Knows the Way Through the Wilderness.") On Thanksgiving night, while he listened to Sidney Cox preach the Gospel, Dad trusted Jesus Christ as his Savior.

The way Dad tells it, his first memory of the woman who would become my mother was that she was a little girl in pigtails sitting in the choir giggling. She had a friend who, like Mom, was named Martha. Dad thought they were always laughing and never had a serious moment.

Mom and Dad both graduated from Middleburg Joint High School, but the two of them had no interest in each other until after Dad's graduation, when Mom was a senior. That year, Dad spotted her at a local carnival. As his interest developed, he finally worked up the courage to ask her for a date for the following Saturday night. She worked at the local five-and-dime, and he just about swallowed his heart when he learned she was scheduled to work until 9:00 that Saturday evening. But Dad always has been quick on his feet, so he asked if he could pick her up after work, and she consented. He thought, *By picking her up at work, I won't have to meet her family!*

What he didn't know was that her folks lived only two doors down from the store. This was the era of socializing on big front porches, and her family had all gathered on the porch to check out the young man who had asked Martha for a date. You can imagine Dad's surprise when he pulled up in front of the store and spotted her father and mother, sister and brother-in-law, and aunt and uncle all waiting to see her go out on her first date.

But Mom says he made a great impression. They all came to like and admire him, and they respected his family— so he won an early approval.

It took Dad about a year to propose to Mom. They were riding around in his old car one day when he told her there was something in the glove compartment for her. She looked in the glove compartment, and there was the engagement ring. They were married January 27, 1956, at the Evangelical United Brethren Church in Middleburg.

Dad was a lot more shy then than he is now. As he tells it, he couldn't even stand up and talk in front of people in the early 1950s. He likes to tell people that he had a lot of complexes, inferiority and otherwise, until that evening in the fall of '53 when he came to know the Lord. Then his complexes just disappeared. Before long my dad was even elected superintendent of the Sunday school here in Kreamer. It seemed like the Lord pushed him into just the right positions to help him get rid of those inhibitions.

Dad has been a huge influence in my life, and I know there were men who influenced him. One was a fellow named Carl Bilger, a godly man who was in the oil business. Dad knew him through the Christian Businessmen's Committee as well as church. He and Dad met together in our home for prayer just about every morning for six years. That was also a big influence on me as I was growing up.

Dad grew up in a Christian home, but Mom's father wasn't involved in church, so her mother took the lead in their family and walked to church with her four children. Mom received Jesus as her Savior at the age of 13 during a fall revival service held in the same church where Dad met the Lord.

Mom once told me she wasn't looking for somebody specific to marry. She had prayed, "Lord, You do the looking, and You send the person." After Dad asked Mom to marry him, she told her family the Lord had reserved him for her. She had always wanted to be a good wife and mother, to have children and be a homemaker. God allowed her to fulfill that.

After he was married, Dad had the privilege of leading Mom's father to Jesus Christ. While talking one night in front of a coal-burning stove, Dad knelt right there in the living room with Grandpa Kleinbauer and prayed with him to receive Christ. I was a little boy back then; it must have been about 1960.

Although Mom's mother died about 25 years ago from breast cancer, her father survived until about 7 years ago. He spent a lot of time riding around with my dad on the truck. Grandpa Kleinbauer became quite ill toward the end of his life. He had diabetes and several other serious medical problems, but Mom and Dad treated him with love and care. Grandpa also had a hearing problem. He had such respect for my dad's prayers, however, that he would say, "I can't always hear what you're praying, but I can feel it."

Grandpa lived with Mom and Dad for a year and a half before he died. I can't help thinking that the way my parents and the rest of our family rallied around him during his illness helped prepare us for the ordeal we were about to experience with my cancer. My sister Tammy, who is a nurse, helped my folks with his care, and all the love and support from the rest of the family helped him feel loved and at home.

* * *

I was the firstborn in our family. Tammy was born three years later. We had a lot of fun growing up in our household, but sometimes we got carried away. One Christmas Eve Tammy and I got into a talcum powder battle in the bathroom. We scattered powder over a big part of the house that evening, but Mom laid down the law and made us clean it up.

I always felt protective of Tammy, even though like most brothers I teased her and my other sisters a lot. In fact, there were plenty of times when I said the wrong thing and insulted my sisters, so I wound up knocking on their bedroom door to apologize and ask forgiveness. I think the Lord used growing up with four sisters to prepare me to get along with a wife and four daughters!

When Tammy started school, I tried to make sure she always made it to class. Then I would meet her after her classes and see that she caught the bus for home. We attended school in Middleburg until we were in the sixth or seventh grade. Although I graduated from Middleburg Joint High School, Tammy and my other sisters wound up attending a Christian school in Kreamer.

While attending Middleburg High School, I crossed paths with Heidi Grove for the first time. We hardly knew each other and didn't dream we would one day be married. But Heidi tells me she had a friend who attended Middleburg, and she would periodically check in with this friend to see if I was dating anyone. I was a year ahead of her in school, so I was at Messiah College during her senior year. When she went to Messiah, I already had quit college to come home and work with Dad.

Then one day, just like Mom and Dad, we met at a local carnival. Our meeting happened in Kreamer, though, rather than in Middleburg. Heidi's cousin was a good friend of Tammy's, so the girls all got together and came to the carnival. I was working at the carnival selling French fries when we were introduced. By the time the evening was over, we had both begun thinking about each other. But I guess I was a little shy, like Dad, and I didn't quite get up the nerve to ask her to let me take her home from the carnival.

Heidi had an aunt and uncle who tried to play cupid. They showed me her picture and encouraged me to date her— but that just made me even more reluctant!

Now that I think about it, though, I'd been hearing about Heidi for some time. Mom and Dad had heard of her as well. She had been chosen valedictorian of her senior class and had given a very emotional and spiritual speech. Mom and Dad somehow secured a copy of the tape and listened to her personal testimony. They admired her for speaking up for the Lord in front of such a large crowd. They suggested to me, "Chris, you really ought to date this girl." In fact, one Sunday on the way to church, Dad pulled out a picture of her and said, "Here she is."

To be honest, the picture didn't make me want to date her. Now that I look back on it, I'm sure it didn't do her justice.

After I met her, what really attracted me to Heidi was her wonderful spirit. Sure, she's good looking, but what a personality!

Finally one Sunday I invited her out. She was home from college, and it was near the end of the summer. I had called her on Saturday night but didn't get her. Then on Sunday I reached her right after the morning church ser-vice and asked if I could take her out two hours later! She agreed— surprisingly, for such short notice— and we went

27

out to play tennis. I found myself really attracted to her, and the better I got to know her, the more I liked her.

Then I realized that in about a week Heidi was headed back to college. Of all the times for her to be going back to school. That school year I kept finding different reasons to drive down to Messiah for weekend visits, soccer games, that sort of thing.

Things progressed in our relationship to the point where, by the following Christmas, Heidi expected us to get engaged, since we had been discussing engagement for some time. So I decided to surprise her before Christmas arrived.

The night before Thanksgiving I picked her up at college. We had taken a special photo of the two of us, and I had a copy enlarged for her. I gave her that and a homemade card. She opened the card, and on the inside was a ring tied with a piece of yarn with a question written beside it— "Will you marry me?"

She said yes!

We always have a Wednesday evening service at church the night before Thanksgiving, and a get-together at my parents' house afterward. Heidi didn't know I had planned for her parents and our grandparents to be there. She thought it was a private occasion, so she slipped the ring off her finger before we walked in, thinking just my parents would be there and I wouldn't have told them.

Then when she walked in and spotted all her family, she realized what it was— an engagement party!

A year later we were married on August 4, 1979, at Kreamer Bible Baptist Church, near the lumberyard. Our first daughter, Emily, was born about three and a half years after we married. Our other girls— Lindsey, Leah and Audrey— arrived about every two and a half years after that. Just about the time one got out of diapers we'd have another one!

* * *

Two other things stand out in my mind about my family. One is the fact that, many years before Heidi and I married, her grandfather, Eugene Grove, and my grandfather, Carson Bingaman, used to get together and drive up into the hills above Kreamer to pray. They were both active in the Christian Businessmen's Committee and seemed to hit it off really well. They would drive into the hills on a dirt road off Highway 522, the main road that runs through Kreamer, then sit there in the car looking over Middle Creek Valley and pray for our family, for our churches, and for the community in general.

The other amazing thing is how Heidi bonded with my sister Mary Beth. Since Heidi and I became one flesh in Christ when we married and since I would ultimately receive the life-giving bone marrow transplant from Mary Beth, it was as though God were letting us know in advance how special she would be.

Looking back on it all, I can see the promise of God's presence even before I came to "the valley of the shadow of death." The way Heidi's grandpa and mine prayed together, the way God brought Mom and Dad together, then brought Heidi and me together and helped her bond with Mary Beth—there's no way I can deny that He was with us every step of the way.

Chapter 3

New Year's Day, 1992

Sometimes you can point to one day in your life that becomes a turning point. Things are pretty much the same up until that day, but from then on everything is different.

New Year's Day, 1992, was that kind of day for me. It's appropriate that it was cold and cloudy, for it was the day I came down with the pneumonia that led to my diagnosis of cancer.

Early in the day we had invited some friends, the Goodlings, over to our home to celebrate the New Year. We had all been down helping Dad on the farm, and I finally said, "Hey, I need to go up to the house. I'm gettin' chills. I'm so cold I can't get warm." So I headed up to our house by myself to try to warm up. Later my friends walked up from Dad's place to our house.

Heidi and I live in a beautiful country home, five miles west of the Susquehanna River in Pennsylvania. I don't think anybody lives in a more gorgeous setting. We can look out from our home over hills and trees and farms in the Middle Creek Valley. Shade Mountain is located just south of us, and Jack's Mountain is to the north.

Our home was constructed of stonework and wooden siding by Heidi's father, Clair Grove, and her uncles Jim and Lawrence Grove. It's a colonial design, and we purposely left it somewhat rustic on the inside. We have a family room with a stone fireplace where we spend most of our time when we are indoors. Since we are in the lumber business, as you might expect, we have hardwood floors. Out back is a deck with tables where we enjoy eating whenever the weather allows. The deck also provides a perfect perch from which to watch for wildlife. We've seen bear, deer, foxes— even flocks of turkeys right in our backyard.

The house is set on a 136-acre farm, where my dad keeps 50 head of beef cattle. Every now and then our girls will scream, "The cows are out and they are in our yard!" We have a chocolate Labrador named Mocha, who chases them back and helps keep things in order.

Dad's primary reason for purchasing so much land was because he had five children, and he figured this would enable him to give each of the children a place to build on. His dad had done the same thing for him and Mom, helping them purchase a lot.

My dad knew about the land and was aware it was for sale. One day 19 years ago he took me to look the place over. We walked up on the hill together where the house is built now. Dad had been thinking about buying the property, but he never said anything to me. When we reached the top of the rise and looked out across the valley, Dad said, "Wouldn't this be a beautiful lot for you to build on?" All I could say was, "Oh, man, Dad."

I fell in love with that spot the first time I saw it. Since I was the oldest and had married first, I got first choice. As Heidi sometimes says, there are advantages to being firstborn!

But back to New Year's Day. It was around lunchtime when I climbed the hill to the house, went indoors, and took a hot shower. Then I got into bed and pulled the quilts around me, trying to get warm, but I just couldn't shake off the chills.

Around 4:30 that afternoon, it was time for our annual New Year's Day dinner. We have a family tradition of serving pork and sauerkraut on January 1. Our friends and Heidi had prepared the meal, and I came downstairs to eat.

By that time I had begun to feel a little better, and I told Heidi so. We ate lots of pork and sauerkraut, and after the Goodlings left, I stayed up and watched a college football bowl game. Penn State, my favorite team, was trouncing its opponent. But as I sat watching the game, I started feeling really sick again, so I went to bed.

I shouldn't be feeling sick, I thought. *I'm in great shape— in fact, the best shape of my life.* I had been climbing a lot, working out, and I prided myself on being physically fit.

Since we live at the top of a hill, there's a steep grade from our house down into a pasture, which is in a ravine. Dad keeps his cattle there much of the time, so it's grazed off. One of my main physical workouts is to climb up and down that hill. Sometimes I'll climb it 20 or 25 times a week. In between those climbs, I regularly jog and lift weights. Of all of my workout activities, the climbing is what I like least, but I do it because it is the hardest.

At the time, I was jogging an average of 10 to 12 miles a week, usually a mile and a half to 3 miles at a time, four days a week. I exercised so much because my job didn't allow me much physical activity, and I felt it was important to keep my body toned. Now I realize my physical condition was extremely important to me, probably too important. I know the Bible says bodily exercise profits a little, but one of the lessons I've learned is that things like physical health and well-being can be taken away very quickly.

By about 2:00 A.M., January 2, I was really sick— probably sicker than I had ever been. I woke Heidi up, and we called Mom and Dad. Then we headed to the hospital in Lewisburg.

The Lewisburg Evangelical Hospital is not very large by big-city standards. It's a three-story brick building with about 300 beds, located in a town about 25 minutes from where we live. Like a lot of hospitals, new wings have been added to it several times. The rooms are quite small.

Mom stayed with the children while Dad and Heidi took me to the hospital, where I was immediately admitted. They put me in a double room with another man. The first couple of days I was there I didn't know much about what was happening. They went by like a blur because I was so sick.

Although the illness struck on New Year's Day, my health the week before had been below par. I remember playing in a pick-up basketball game at work a couple of days before Christmas Eve. (In one of the warehouses we've set up a basketball court. Several of us like to play at lunchtime.) That day every time I tried to jump, it was like my wind was taken away, and there was a terrible pain in my back. I went home from work in the middle of the day, then decided to take a couple of days off and rest.

By Christmas I was feeling a bit better, so I came downstairs that morning and lifted weights. I actually thought that would help me feel better, but lifting weights made things much worse. In fact, on Christmas my back was worse than ever. From Christmas until New Year's, my back pain was a constant irritation. Later I found out that not only did I have pneumonia, caused by the cancer that was affecting my immune system, I also had a collapsed vertebrae.

I don't recall a lot about my stay in the Lewisburg hospital. A couple of doctors saw me, but when I didn't recover quickly, they called in a third doctor, an ear, nose and throat specialist. Dr. Bruce really seemed to know his business. He was tall with brown eyes and thick, brown hair, a bushy mustache and a great sense of humor. But he wasn't joking the day he came in and said, "They just called me in on your case. They are a little concerned about the fact that you are not recovering. We'd like to go in and do a bronchoscopy." This was on the Saturday after I entered the hospital.

Dr. Bruce explained the procedure, then said, "Now we're going to take you to the operating room." At that point I was really concerned. What exactly are they looking for?

They wheeled me into the operating room, gave me an injection in the throat, then went down my esophagus with a tube. I was awake during the whole procedure. Dr. Bruce kept talking to me, saying things like, "I'm in your right lung now; that's looking good." A couple of minutes later he said, "Oh, your left lung looks good too." I was glad when they finally pulled the tubes out and took me back to my room. What a relief to be assured that my lungs were healthy! The whole procedure took only 15 or 20 minutes, but it seemed like half a lifetime.

After that they ran some additional tests. Finally I started improving. My fever broke, and before long I was sent home. On my way back to the house, we stopped to pick up some prescription antibiotics.

Though my lungs looked good, the nagging pain in my back hadn't left and that created lingering doubts in my mind. I had mentioned it to the doctors and their response was, "Well, since you had pneumonia, it's probably from your lungs." I went to bed thinking, *It's so good to be back home in my own bed.* But during the night the back pain hit again. It was so bad I had to get up, go downstairs and sit in the La-Z-Boy recliner.

After a couple of days of no relief, I called one of the doctors at the family practice center and explained my predicament to him. "I want you to come in right away," he told me. "We'll get some X rays." So I did. They x-rayed me, and everything looked fine. The doctor told me, "You probably have pleurisy." He gave me some anti-inflammatory medication and said, "Take that. This should clear things up in a couple of days."

Little did I know how unclear my condition really was.

Chapter 4

What's My Problem?

Before I was diagnosed with pneumonia on New Year's Day, I was probably in the best physical shape of my life. Yet that didn't keep me from having severe pain in my back and rib cage, a pain that never went away, even after I was over my pneumonia. The doctors at our local medical clinic— and several of them had seen me— thought my pain was caused by pleurisy.

On January 27, my daughter Emily's birthday, I had come downstairs to check on the fire. On my way back upstairs, I stopped at the refrigerator for a drink. Suddenly, the pain hit me so sharply I couldn't breathe. I was crawling up the steps when Heidi heard me faintly cry out for help. I told her I couldn't get my breath. She felt as much panic as I did and immediately dialed 911. I was rushed to the hospital by ambulance, but after the doctor checked me over, he assured me the problem was pleurisy. Again, I was given a prescription for prednisone, an anti-inflammatory medication, and sent home.

I couldn't have guessed at that time what an important role prednisone would later play in helping me through my ongoing cancer treatment. I've been an athlete for most of my life, playing soccer competitively and enjoying other sports such as basketball. One of the first lessons you learn in sports is the importance of playing through pain. Never was that more obvious than in the 1996 Summer Olympics when U.S. gymnast Kerri Strug sprained her foot vaulting. Then she attempted a second vault— the one that won her team the gold medal— and when she landed on that twisted ankle, it was obvious how much pain she was in. But she bore it willingly for the sake of her team.

Her coach had encouraged her—and others did as well—and she turned in a gritty performance. I can relate to her efforts because when my back hurt so badly, I determined to "play through" my pain.

In addition, I'm an optimistic person, so whenever I'd start feeling a little better, I'd think, *I'm finally pulling out of this. I'm getting better. The pain is still there, but it's not as bad.*

I recall one trip I made with Dad down to Maryland for business. As we drove along, Dad kept expressing a lot of concern, and I said, "Boy, I think I'm feeling better today, Dad." The whole trip we were both rejoicing because we thought I was getting better.

But that night, after the trip, the pain returned with a vengeance! I'd been taking prednisone for several weeks by then with no apparent results. It was time to find out what was really wrong.

I guess that's part of the value of pain. In some ways it's like the red warning light on the dashboard of a car—it lets you know when something is wrong. Reading about Paul's thorn in the flesh in 2 Corinthians 12 encouraged me. His pain wasn't without purpose. God allowed it to help him see an underlying problem. In these situations, people sometimes go to one of two extremes: They either deny they are hurting, grit their teeth and try to pretend it's not that bad, or they simply look for a way to kill the pain without dealing with its underlying cause. I certainly wanted to get rid of my pain, but in hindsight I realize how important it was that we got to the bottom of what was causing my back to keep hurting.

I'm convinced that the Lord had just the right person to help me deal with my pain. His name was Dr. John Weston, and I believe God sent him to our church to be the means by which I would discover the cause of all my pain.

Several years before my cancer, Dr. Weston moved to our area, set up a medical practice and started attending our church. In time I came to know him as a friend and fellow church member. He had visited me as a friend but not professionally on a couple of earlier occasions when I was sick.

Dr. Weston is one of the kindest men I've ever met. He's about 40 years old, tall with blonde hair and striking good looks. He is also a very thorough physician. When I was hospitalized in January 1992, Dr. Weston came by to see me, and I asked if he would take me as a new patient. He reluctantly agreed to do so, saying, "Chris, I don't want you to feel like you should be seeing me as your physician just because we're friends." He and I agreed that the doctors at the family practice center were good. But I expressed my concern that this was my second round of pneumonia, and I was always seeing different doctors from the center. I had talked things over with Heidi and with my parents as well. Everybody was in favor of Dr. Weston because we all knew him.

After I was discharged from the hospital but not getting any better, I phoned and asked him if I could see him. When I told him I was still in a lot of pain, Dr. Weston expressed a great deal of concern and set up an appointment for me the next morning.

During that visit, he ran all kinds of tests, including a number of different blood tests and an X ray of my lungs. When I asked him why he was repeating some of the tests that I'd had earlier, Dr. Weston replied, "I think we need to have a new baseline to work from. I want to find out exactly what's going on here." In addition to the other tests, he said he wanted to do a bone scan. Obviously, he suspected that there was something more to this than just pain. That visit was the first time the word *cancer* came up. "I'm not trying to scare you, Chris," Dr. Weston said. "I just want you to know all the possibilities."

I must confess that I, too, had thought about cancer. When I was in the hospital earlier and had undergone the bronchoscopy, it occurred to me that the doctors might be looking for evidence of cancer. I don't smoke, but I wondered if by some fluke I had developed lung cancer. But when Dr. Bruce declared my lungs healthy, I pretty well dismissed cancer from my thinking.

As my pain persisted, however, I returned to Dr. Weston's office for more blood work and a change in medication. He tried prednisone again; then after another visit he switched me to a different anti-inflammatory medication for the pleurisy. Each time the improvement seemed to last a week or so. During these brief periods I kept thinking I was getting better.

On my third visit to Dr. Weston's office, he again expressed his concern over my inability to improve. I know now he was suspicious of multiple myeloma, but at that time the term meant nothing to me. Of course, the word *cancer* did! During that Thursday morning visit, he ordered several more tests, including a series of side view X rays of my back. After completing the tests, I returned to my office.

While I was at the office that afternoon, Dr. Weston called to inform me that the X rays showed a collapsed vertebrae in my back. He began to question me about whether I had fallen or had been in some kind of collision that might have caused such an injury. I told him I couldn't think of anything. He then suggested I come over to his office first thing next morning, a Friday. As I hung up the phone, I was overwhelmed with relief. Dr. Weston had finally found the cause of my pain. Surely I must be on the road to recovery at last!

Right away I walked over to Dad's office to tell him the news. While standing there discussing the call, however, I began to feel one of my usual spasms of pain. I was forced to lie down on his office floor to get some relief before we could finish our conversation.

As I drove to the hospital that Friday morning, I was filled with intense thankfulness that my problem had finally been identified, and I felt confident I would soon be feeling better. The day was sunny and warm— certainly not typical for February in Pennsylvania. As I steered my Jeep Wagoneer across the bridge in New Berlin, I kept praying over and over, "Thank You, Lord. I may have a broken vertebrae, but at least they know what's wrong." But that was to be the high point of my emotions for the day.

After I arrived at the hospital, I was given a series of tests, including another bone scan and a series of CAT scans. Later that afternoon, when I returned to Dr.

Weston's office, Tammy, his secretary, informed me that the doctor intended to have me admitted to the hospital immediately. My heart sank in discouragement.

Chapter 5

Cancer and
Its Treatment

Back in 1913, when the American Cancer Society was founded, most people considered cancer a death sentence. During the 1930s fewer than 20 percent of cancer patients were still alive five years after their initial treatment. Today that number is up to 50 percent.

Approximately one million new cases of cancer are diagnosed each year in the United States. This includes everything from breast cancer, which affects one out of nine women, to prostate cancer, which affects an additional 100,000 men each year.

Cancer can strike anyone— those with healthy lifestyles as well as those who increase their risks by smoking, eating the wrong kinds of foods and consuming alcohol. And there's no way to know who will get cancer or even always a reason why its victims get it. After all, the human body is a remarkable creation. God designed us with hundreds of muscles, billions of cells, miles and miles of blood vessels and nerves, and a complex array of chemicals. Like the psalmist put it, we are "fearfully and wonderfully made" (Psalm 139:14).

We also live in a fallen world. I guess it would be accurate to say that cancer ultimately affects people because of sin. That certainly doesn't mean everyone's cancer is a direct result of sinful behavior, but research done by the National Cancer Institute indicates that diet and tobacco play a major role in almost two-thirds of all cancer deaths. Other key factors today include sexual relations, particularly outside marriage, as well as alcohol consumption. Infection, stress, exposure to sunshine and radiation, and pollution also put people at risk of cancer.

The way I've heard cancer described is that something— maybe a virus or an environmental factor— causes the genes in our cells to take a "hit". These hits build up over time until finally a cell becomes malignant.

Once this happens, malignant cells begin to multiply rapidly. One abnormal cell becomes two, then four. In fact, some fast-growing cancers may double in size in a matter of weeks. Other tumors may grow for years before they are detected.

The researchers at the Arkansas Cancer Research Center, where I eventually was treated, have carried on an extensive investigation of multiple myeloma, the cancer I was diagnosed with. They are on the cutting edge of clinical research into this particular malignancy.

I read an article from the *New England Journal of Medicine* that said there's been very little change in the treatment of multiple myeloma since the introduction of what's known as the "melphalan-prednisone" regimen about 25 years ago. I felt a little strange reading that article since one of my physicians, Dr. Barlogie, was the primary author. According to Dr. Barlogie, doses of melphalan, given at toxic levels, have consistently produced a complete remission of cancers like mine in 20 to 30 percent of patients. Those numbers are based on the collective experience of more than 350 reported cases of autologous bone marrow transplants. According to these statistics, fewer than 5 percent of those so treated died, and more than 30 percent experienced a complete remission. Thus, the treatment of choice is an autologous bone marrow transplant coupled with intense chemotherapy. That's also what my physicians told me.

I was frightened by the description of multiple myeloma in this article. It was described as "a currently incurable cancer in which the median survival does not exceed three years." Those are just words on a page, but when you have been diagnosed with multiple myeloma, it hits you pretty hard. As I continued reading I discovered that almost 40 percent of the patients treated with a transplant of a donor's bone marrow— the term they use is allogeneic—died of treatment-related complications within the first three to four months after the transplant. Reading that felt like a kick in the stomach!

However, when I read that 40 percent of those treated with this kind of transplant were projected to be alive after five years, and the median duration of relapse-free survival was four years, I began to feel better.

One of the side benefits—if you could call it that—of having cancer is you tend to be motivated to do a lot of reading on the subject. I discovered cancers like multiple myeloma are linked to genetic defects.

We've all heard the term *genes* used many times without fully understanding what we mean. According to Dr. Richard Hoover, director of the Molecular Diagnosis Laboratory at the Arkansas Cancer Research Center, genes are hereditary units made up of molecules called deoxyribonucleic acid. You're probably more familiar with the abbreviation DNA.

Everyone has two sets of genes. We inherited one set from our mother and the other from our father. Genes are responsible for all our physical characteristics, including eye and hair color. Some recent studies suggest that even some of our behavior may be influenced by genes. Clearly, our genetic makeup has a major influence on our lives, including whether or not we develop a disease such as cancer.

While there are some diseases that are inherited directly, such as cystic fibrosis, most cancers aren't a direct result of a defective gene. There are some exceptions—for example, a rare form of tumor of the eye, called retinoblastoma, is inherited. Most genetic traits are stable throughout our lifetimes.

However, environmental influences may cause our genes to become damaged. Most people are aware of some of the environmental dangers that can lead to this, including cigarette smoke—both for smokers and secondary smoke for nonsmokers—plus ultraviolet rays from the sun and even exposure to large doses of radiation, such as those that occur in nuclear accidents.

The Arkansas Cancer Research Center established the Molecular Diagnosis Laboratory to investigate the structure and function of damaged genes that may cause cancer. Scientists there use state-of-the-art techniques in molecular biology to examine blood and tissue samples to detect the presence and function of known cancer-causing genes. Most of the tests they perform are on the cutting edge of basic clinical science and are not generally available to the medical community at large. That's one reason why I'm thankful I discovered the ACRC, since it was able to provide a much more detailed tumor characterization than what is typically available from conventional diagnostic techniques. Throughout my treatment, ACRC staff were also able to check me for the presence of what are called "marker genes," which help determine whether or not a tumor has changed during treatment. Information from these genes allows the clinicians to make appropriate changes in the treatment process.

At this point, however, Arkansas was still ahead of me. Right now I needed to deal with a more imminently threatening medical situation— a collapsed vertebrae that could leave me paralyzed!

Chapter 6

Divine Providence

I was admitted to the hospital on a Friday and given a semiprivate room. I lay in the bed next to the window; a student from Bucknell University occupied the other bed. He had been there for a day or two, hospitalized because of some kind of seizure.

What followed was a weekend that seemed to last forever—occasional tests interspersed with a great deal of time to think. On Saturday morning I was taken to X ray for a complete body scan.

On the following Monday the weather turned gray and dreary. Drizzling rain streaked the window, and it seemed like the sun would never shine again. Early that morning, the technicians took me down to the first floor for an MRI. It can be a frightening procedure. I was laid out flat, then rolled into this huge, tunnel-like contraption.

Following the MRI I became rather upset when the nurses wouldn't allow me to sit up. One nurse kept saying, "You've got to stay flat; you have to keep lying down." They used pillows to brace my head securely in place, then moved me gingerly to the stretcher to take me back to my room. A man came in with a huge brace for my back. I had no idea what was going on.

About an hour later Dr. Weston walked in. He looked at my chart and said, "Chris, we've checked your MRI. It shows you have a collapsed vertebrae pinching your spinal cord." He echoed my thoughts when he said, "This is very serious, and you're going to need surgery to repair your back."

At that moment the phone rang. As he reached over to pick up the phone, Dr. Weston said, "It's probably for me. I told them to page me here." After he listened for a moment, he grabbed my chart and started writing. I remember his words vividly: "Give me the normal first, then give me Chris's." After he had written several numbers down, he said, "OK, that's all I need. Thank you."

When he hung up the phone he said, "Well, this pretty well confirms it. You have multiple myeloma."

It almost sounds trite to say I was in shock, but that's exactly how I felt. I was numb all over. I knew I'd been hit hard, but it was too early for me to tell how hard. I was still trying to process the fact that I had cancer. I didn't feel strongly optimistic, as in "I'm sure I'll beat this," or depressed, feeling "This will probably get me." I was still groping to grasp the whole reality of it.

That same morning, Heidi took Audrey to her parents' house, then dropped Lindsey and Leah off at a friend of ours, Holly Follmer's. Afterwards she met my mom and dad in the hospital parking lot, and the three of them came up to my room. I was lying in a back brace with orders to stay in bed. I think Mom and Dad had already begun to suspect that I had cancer. When I told them, their worst fears were confirmed. I could see apprehension on their faces even as we joined together in prayer. Dad, Mom and Heidi knelt there beside my bed— right in the room with the college student— and they asked the Lord to heal me and to give us the wisdom regarding where to go for treatment.

That's one of the things I've learned through this battle. You pray as though everything depends on God, but you pursue the very best medical care as though it's all up to you. Those two things aren't inconsistent at all. It's like the story about a man who was in a rowboat in the middle of a lake when a thunderstorm hit. As he later described it, "You do two things when you are in that situation. You pray hard, and you row to shore."

After my family and I prayed together, I recall two predominant feelings— and they seemed contradictory. On the one hand, I began to really feel the Lord's presence.

There wasn't any particular reason for it, but I just felt a confidence, a trust, that I would be okay. I prayed, "Lord, I just want to know Your way for me."

But at that same time I began wrestling with questions like, "Lord, are You really there?"

I know Heidi must have been afraid, too, but what impressed me the most about her at that point was her quiet confidence and the smile on her face after we prayed. She referred to Isaiah 40:31, "Those that wait on the Lord will renew their strength," and she said, "Chris, I still believe God's going to restore you."

After our prayer time, Dad phoned Dr. Weston. He had told me to tell my folks to feel free to get in touch with him if they had any questions.

I wasn't surprised when Dad asked, "Dr. Weston, if this were your son, what would you do?" Now, Dr. Weston already had told me he wanted to send me up to Divine Providence Hospital in Williamsport. He had recommended Dr. Rodwan Rajjoub, a highly respected surgeon, to operate on my back. He was also very positive about its oncology department.

Dad mentioned several options to Dr. Weston, including Memorial Sloan-Kettering, and some other well-known hospitals that specialize in cancer treatment. As Dad explained later, Dr. Weston didn't mince words with his reply. He said, "Max, if this were my son, I would do exactly what I recommended to Chris." At that point we felt this was the direction we should go.

Late that evening, Heidi still had some misgivings, even though the decision had been made that I was going to Divine Providence in Williamsport. I was to be transferred by ambulance at 7:00 the next morning. Heidi and Mom would follow the ambulance by car, and Dad would drive up later. That evening after Mom, Dad and Heidi had reached the decision for me to go to Divine Providence, Heidi talked with some of her family members. She made a couple of other calls to some people who were knowledgeable in the medical field, and they told her how experienced the staff of another local hospital, the Geisinger Hospital, was in dealing with cancer. Heidi's dad also was extremely concerned and thought we ought to consider that option. (His advice wasn't given to complicate our decision, but because of the tremendous love he and Carolyn have for Heidi and me, which they demonstrated again and again throughout this ordeal. Heidi's parents and her two sisters, Tracy and Angie, provided incredible support. Her dad helped with many things around the house, and my mother-in-law was there for us in more ways than I could begin to describe.)

Later that same evening, Heidi phoned my dad and asked, "What do you think? Shall we go to Geisinger or Divine Providence?" After they talked, they agreed that they had asked the Lord for wisdom, and they felt the direction they had decided was still the right one. As Dad put it, "When we get Chris to Divine Providence, if we feel like any doors aren't opening, we can always reevaluate our decision."

I was transported to Divine Providence the following morning and spent about three hours in surgery the next day. Dr. Rajjoub removed about a one-inch piece of my vertebrae as well as numerous bone fragments. The surgery confirmed what we already suspected— the multiple myeloma was the cause of my collapsed vertebrae. Within a week after the surgery, my back was pain-free except for a few post-surgical twinges.

Looking back, I'm convinced that God had given my "central committee"— Heidi, Dad and Mom— the wisdom they needed when they asked Him. They did precisely what James 1:5 tells us to do— ask for wisdom, and ask in faith. God's presence and His wisdom were guiding us every step of the way.

Chapter 7

A Needle
in My Spine

March 31, 1992, dawned sunny and cold. I felt appre-
hensive as we drove to Divine Providence Hospital for
my first bone marrow aspiration. But everything went
smoothly, and I returned home that afternoon. The
back surgery confirmed that I had a tumor. Now it was
important to determine whether or not my bone marrow
was involved.

Dr. Rajjoub, who performed the operation on my spine,
became our surgeon of choice— a decision that Heidi, Dad
and Mom agonized over. But Dad had received a phone
call from Heidi's father earlier, and we all felt better
because he discovered that Dr. Rajjoub had been on a
team of consulting physicians who were called upon to
give advice to the surgeon who operated on President
Reagan and James Brady when they were shot at the
Washington Hilton Hotel in 1981. I remember Dad saying,
"If he's good enough for the president, he's certainly good
enough for my son."

The bone marrow aspiration didn't take long, about
half an hour. I was given a local anesthetic, then they
went into the pelvic region and up into the spine with a
needle that seemed about as thick as a drinking straw. It
really wasn't, but it was about six inches long and
encased in a cylindrical housing unit. The procedure is
called aspiration because some of the marrow is sucked
out of the spine. They also withdrew a piece of the bone
itself to test.

I was very impressed with my oncologist, Dr. Johannes
Blom, an older, tall, silver-haired man originally from

Holland. He was both kind and gracious. During my first trip to Williamsport for my back surgery, he had been one of the first physicians to visit me. I recall how he described the treatment options and explained, "We'll go through about 30 days of radiation, Chris. Then we'll do this bone marrow draw." When I pressed him and asked, "Doc, what if there is cancer in my bone marrow?" he didn't give me many answers at the time. Now I realize why he didn't. I'm sure he was holding off telling me about the possibility of a bone marrow transplant.

The following Thursday, April 2, we were waiting for Dr. Blom's call. When it came time for my radiation treatment, we drove the eight miles to the radiation clinic in Hummels Wharf, realizing that Dr. Blom might call there. Following the treatment, I mentioned that I still hadn't heard anything from Dr. Blom. One of the nurses said, "Why don't we call him now and see if they have your test results?" As I stood there in the nurses' area outside the room where they gave me the radiation treatments, someone said, "Chris, Dr. Blom is on the phone."

I picked up the telephone, and the words I heard will be etched forever in my memory: "Chris, unfortunately your bone marrow is involved."

Many times I have reflected upon my feelings at that moment, and there's only one word to describe them—death. Up until then I had remained mostly upbeat. I figured I was in for a tough battle, but I thought I was up to the challenge. Yet when Dr. Blom told me my bone marrow was involved, I felt like I'd been hit in the stomach with a sledgehammer. *Man, I'm in big, big trouble.*

The Bible says it's appointed unto man once to die; I had read those words from Hebrews 9:27 many times. But when you are young, have a wife and children, a good job, a nice home and you've been healthy and felt good for as long as I had, you just don't think about death. That's something that happens only to older people, or those who are unfortunate enough to be taken in an accident or in some other untimely fashion.

Now all of a sudden I was one of those people—I had a good chance of becoming a statistic, someone who died before his time.

By now I had learned enough about cancer to know that when your bone marrow is involved, things look pretty grim. I held the telephone receiver and looked at Heidi. She could tell from the look on my face what was going through my mind. She just put her arms around me and held me while I talked to the doctor. That's the kind of encouraging wife she is— no sermons, no fake words of cheer. She just held me and let me know she was there with me, no matter what.

Dr. Blom must have known what I was thinking, for he immediately said, "Chris, would you consider going for a bone marrow transplant?" I didn't have to think about my reply. I just said, "Doctor, I'll consider anything I can do to get well."

He asked if I would be willing to travel, and I said, "Sure, anywhere you think I ought to go." He replied, "Let me make a few phone calls and get back to you." Then he hung up. I stood there for a minute shaking my head, feeling numb all over. It was the biggest reality check of my relatively young life.

But what I didn't know was that the providence of God was already at work. I'd find out more about that the next day.

When Heidi and I left the radiation clinic after learning the news, we knew everybody was anxiously awaiting the results. We felt wiped out. We knew we had to go home and tell them that things were much more serious than we had thought. One reason we felt so disappointed was that so many people were praying. The elders from our church had been over to our home and prayed with me, and we all expected God would answer with good news.

As soon as we returned home, I drove over to the office and hurried upstairs to see Dean Heintzelman, my uncle and our vice president of operations. He called our office manager, Scott Shaffer, and some of the other close people in our organization into the office so I could tell them what the doctors had told me.

Our company headquarters is a two-story, gable-roofed building. It doesn't look anything like a traditional office building. It actually resembles a home in some ways. Our offices are on the second floor. Mine isn't very big, about 10' by 12', but since we are in the lumber business, we all have some of the nicest wood you can imagine. I have cherry paneling and a cherry desk. Dad's office— the largest on the floor, of course— has walnut paneling, an oak desk and a conference table. Dean's office has a walnut desk with walnut paneling.

We all gathered in Dean's office, and I shared the news. I can't remember the exact words I used, but everybody seemed moved. All the staff members, secretaries and others came in. People hugged me and shared my grief. I sensed a great deal of support, but I still felt discouraged.

Right after that meeting, I went out to our van with Heidi to drive home. The reality of the news began to soak into my mind and emotions, and I felt overwhelmed. Uncle Dean followed me out to the van. As I started to get into the car, Dean put his strong arm around my shoulder and with tears in his eyes said, "Chris, I've known you ever since you were small. I played basketball against you, hunted with you and worked with you. I know you're a fighter. Don't give up now. Fight this cancer with the same determination you've had in the past." His words, coming from an uncle I respected so highly, a man of few words who seldom showed emotion, were a ray of hope on an otherwise ominous day.

Mom and Dad weren't there the day I found out my bone marrow was involved. They had flown to Colorado Springs for a Focus on the Family conference. That afternoon they called from the airport in Chicago, where they were waiting for their flight to Harrisburg. They wanted to know if I knew anything and how I was doing. They talked to Scott Shaffer. Dad told me later they could tell from the way Scott's voice cracked that something was very wrong. Mom and Dad felt devastated. They had been so hopeful for good results and that the radiation treatments would end my battle with cancer. But it wasn't to be.

We decided it would be best for our whole family to drive down to Harrisburg to meet Mom and Dad at the airport. I don't remember much about what we said on the way. It's a beautiful drive along the Susquehanna River, but my mind was a long way from the beauty of God's creation at that point. I just wondered what was coming. What did we face? Would I even be around for my next birthday?

When Mom and Dad stepped off the plane, I could tell they were glad the whole family was there. Heidi and I, though, stood at the back. I'm sure they could sense by looking at us, and by the way we hung back, how devastated we were by the news.

Later when I talked to Dad, I realized he had been doing a lot of thinking on the flight from Chicago after he talked with Scott and found out I would need a bone marrow transplant. He had been thinking— and had told Mom— maybe he could give his bone marrow. In fact, she told me later he said he'd be willing to give his life for me. But then that's the kind of dad he is— a lot like the Heavenly Father.

Chapter 8

Rays of Hope

A cord of hope tied together each incident of my battle with cancer. Heidi told me how back in February the Lord had impressed Romans 12:12 on her mind for our situation. It talks about being "joyful in hope, patient in affliction, faithful in prayer." I realized how important hope was for a successful battle with cancer.

Heidi also shared with me how, one Monday morning when she was preparing to take the girls to school, she had prayed, "Lord, I just need to hear from You, and I don't have time to sit down." She turned on the radio and asked Him to speak to her through something. Almost immediately, a song by Mark Lowry came on. The song was titled "There Is Hope." The words of the song read:

> *Sometimes we go through trials that are so hard to bear.*
>
> *We lift our face toward heaven. God, are You really there?*
>
> *I've asked that same question. I've been down that road.*
>
> *Looking back, I contend He always let me know.*
>
> *There is hope. So hold on, there is hope.*
>
> *God sent me here to tell you . . . There is hope.*
>
> *He knows just what you are going through and what the future holds.*

As long as Jesus lives, there is hope.

He was bruised for our transgressions, nailed upon a tree.

He cried out to the Father, "Why have You forsaken Me?"

Through this suffering Savior, He brought healing to our pain.

And the One who raised Him from the dead can restore us once again.

The Lord spoke to Heidi through that song— and through her, to me— that as long as Jesus is alive there is hope.

When we first began planning this book, I talked with Don Hawkins about how important hope is to surviving cancer. He told me about all the different cancer patients he had interviewed when he wrote his first book on the subject, and how they all came to realize that cancer is not an automatic death sentence— that there is hope for survival and even a positive quality of life.

We also discussed how Scripture is filled with evidences of the hope we have in Jesus Christ, and how we can apply this hope to our experience even during the darkest times of life.

For example, David, during some of his worst experiences, reminded himself, "Put your hope in God, for I will yet praise him, my Savior and my God" (Psalm 42:5, 11; 43:5). Jeremiah regained emotional and spiritual perspective during what seemed like a hopeless personal and national disaster by refocusing attention from his own circumstances to God's loyal love and tender compassions. "The Lord is my portion," the prophet wrote, "Therefore I hope in Him!" (Lamentations 3:24, NKJV).

Now those who are not Christians can certainly develop a form of hope, but only those who truly know Christ can experience the living hope that provides the basis for our rebirth. Why? Because that hope is based on the res-urrection of Jesus Christ. According to the apostle Peter, this hope can sustain us through any kind of personal tri-als and adversities (1 Peter 1:3, 6). We can rejoice even in our worst adversities, since we know God's purpose is not to destroy us but to lovingly develop us. That must have been in Paul's mind when he wrote how hope doesn't dis-appoint us because "God has poured out his love into our hearts by the Holy Spirit" (Romans 5:5).

The day after I learned that multiple myeloma had invaded my bone marrow, the darkest day in my life, God provided me with the first of three rays of hope. It occurred when Dr. Blom called. He wondered if I would be willing to go to Little Rock, Arkansas. I felt like saying, "Wait a minute, Doctor. I thought you were looking for the cutting edge of technology. Little Rock, Arkansas? You must be joking."

But Dr. Blom must have been anticipating my con-cerns. He went on to explain that his wife, who also is a physician, had graduated from the University of Arkansas. She had been receiving correspondence about the Arkansas Cancer Research Center and how it special-ized in multiple myeloma. In fact, it was the only center in the United States that specializes in that particular form of cancer. This was not coincidence; it was providence.

After we arrived in Arkansas, many of the other multi-ple myeloma patients would ask, "How in the world did you find out about this place so quickly?" I would reply, "Well, my doctor recommended it." And when they asked, "How did he know?" I couldn't help realizing how God had sent us to Dr. Blom just to get us to this treatment cen-ter right away. Things were dark, and my life was very much at risk. Yet I found hope in the fact that we had learned of a treatment facility that specialized in the can-cer I had.

The second ray of hope happened in one of those little, seemingly coincidental events that had the fingerprint of God all over it.

The Sunday morning before we left for Arkansas, as I was getting ready for church, I thought, *Our future is in such a turmoil. The world around us is collapsing.* As we were about to leave for church—three of the girls were already in the van—Leah, our third daughter, stopped at the front door of our home. "Daddy, come look at these birds!" she exclaimed. Birds? She's certainly not one for bird watching.

First Heidi went over to see what had Leah's attention. When she called out, "Chris, come here," I knew from the tone of her voice there was something I needed to see. I walked over and there on the floor mat beside our French doors stood two doves, a male and a female.

I had never seen doves on our doorstep before, nor have I seen any since. Those doves stood by the door for a long time, then they turned around together and walked away. I never did see them fly. I haven't a clue where they came from, but I have an idea why they were there. It's as though the Lord sent those doves to remind us of His care and the peace He provides. I didn't know what would happen in the days ahead, but the Lord used those doves to remind me of His wise love, His caring presence and His Spirit.

You may be thinking, *Chris, you're reading too much into a small coincidence.* But when I mentioned this incident to Don as we were working on this book, he brought up Zechariah 4:10—one of his favorite verses, but one I was unfamiliar with. The verse says, "Who despises the day of small things?" As I understand it, God was telling the Israelites when they had rebuilt a temple that was much smaller and plainer than Solomon's magnificent structure that it is important to look for His hand in the small, everyday things of life. As I consider all the things that have happened to me over the past few years—and this is just one of many "little things"—I'm convinced I can see the loving, caring hand of God guiding us all the way.

The third ray of hope has to do with running. From January 1, 1992, on, because of the back pain and the pneumonia, I found it necessary to give up jogging, something I really enjoyed. As I mentioned earlier, Heidi told me on the day of the diagnosis, "Chris, I'm praying and believing Isaiah 40:31—you will run again." I looked up that verse and read, "Those who hope in the Lord . . . will run and not grow weary, they will walk and not faint."

When I was told I needed a bone marrow transplant, I didn't even know if I'd live, much less run again.

I remember the first time I was able to run after my back surgery. One Sunday afternoon about four weeks after the operation, but before I learned that the cancer had affected my bone marrow, I was walking on Dad's treadmill in the basement of their home. I decided to turn up the speed and see if I could run. I did, for just a couple of minutes, run again! Dad was there with me, and there were tears in our eyes. God had fulfilled the promise Heidi had claimed, just as He fulfilled all His other promises every step of the way.

At a time when we very easily could have given up hope, God sent those rays of hope to let us know He was right there with us, making certain we knew His hand was upon us and His heart was turned toward us.

Chapter 9

Little Rock

When you face a series of stays in the hospital the way I did, one of your biggest concerns is care for your children. During my initial hospitalization at Divine Providence, my sister Tammy took charge of our girls. She wanted to free Heidi to be with me as much as possible. Staying at Tim and Tammy's was a great experience for our girls. Their children are so close to ours that, in light of the situation, it was the best possible setting for them.

Before we left for our first trip to Little Rock on April 12, 1992, there were two significant events. Friday, the day before we were scheduled to fly out, I picked up the newspaper. There was a picture and a story on the front page. Sam Walton, who started the Wal-Mart chain of stores, had died of multiple myeloma at the University of Arkansas Hospital. He had been one of the "founding fathers" of the Arkansas Cancer Research Center. I thought, *And that's where I'm going for treatment?* Reading that story didn't give me a lot of cause for cheer.

Later that same day, however, my mother shared with me a verse the Lord had impressed on her, Deuteronomy 31:8:

> *The Lord himself goes before you and will be with you; he will never leave you nor forsake you. Do not be afraid; do not be discouraged.*

When I studied that verse further, I discovered how Moses at the age of 120 had given these words of encouragement to Joshua! Israel was about to cross over into the Promised Land, and God told Moses he wouldn't be allowed to go. But the old patriarch had reminded Israel that the Lord would go before them, destroy all the enemies and give them the land He had promised them. In the opening verses of Deuteronomy 31, Moses reminded the Israelites to be strong, courageous and unafraid, since the Lord would be with them. Then he called Joshua, his successor, and gave him the specific promise in verse 8 that Mom claimed for me.

I felt a lot of uncertainty as I packed my suitcase to head for Little Rock. Yet that verse kept going through my mind. The Lord goes before you. He will be with you. He will never leave you nor forsake you. Do not be afraid; do not be discouraged. It's uncanny how the promises of God's Word can sustain us, especially in the face of seemingly hopeless circumstances.

Heidi and I were to fly from Harrisburg to Charlotte, North Carolina, then change planes for the final leg of the trip. Heidi's grandmother flew with us as far as Charlotte, where she had made plans to visit family members. I experienced some pain in my rib cage during the flight, and began spitting up some blood.

All through the flight I kept thinking, *A bone marrow transplant seems like the only hope I have left—and I don't even know if I would be a candidate or if it would be possible.* I arrived in Little Rock with a fair amount of fear—but I felt hopeful too.

Little Rock was sunny, hot and muggy with a warm breeze. We went straight from the airport to a place called the Guest House Inn, located directly across University Avenue from St. Vincent's Hospital. The Inn is run by Tom and Judy Adam.

Tom and Judy have created a home-away-from-home atmosphere to accommodate patients and their families who come to Little Rock for treatment. According to Judy, about 40 percent of the business at the Guest House comes from patients at the Arkansas Cancer Research Center. When nurses at St. Vincent's work double shifts and can't drive home because they live too far away, they frequently stay at the Inn. There's even a room provided on the second floor for a nurse to do blood work on patients.

We came to know Tom and Judy Adam well and considered them family during our five visits to Little Rock. I learned that Tom and Judy had no experience in hotel management before they opened the Guest House, but you would never know it from the way they run the place. Every morning they provide fresh donuts and coffee, and most of all a pleasant, friendly atmosphere.

As soon as we arrived at the Guest House, we were told to head over to the hospital, so we did. My first impressions weren't positive. The hospital was an old building, several stories tall. When I walked inside I thought, *This certainly doesn't appear to be the cleanest hospital I've ever seen.* I was expecting new technology and new equipment, so I felt disappointed, even disillusioned.

We walked into a room where there were a number of people lying on couches. They all looked incredibly sick. Since they were taking chemo and radiation therapy, they also had no hair. I thought, *Oh, my, what am I getting into?*

I handed the nurse my slip, and she said, "We have your paperwork right here." She was a short, slender African-American woman named Diane. She radiated cheerfulness— she was certainly a bright spot in what was otherwise a discouraging first day. She immediately began drawing blood from me. I think Diane wound up taking more than 20 tubes of blood! I jokingly asked her, "How many gallons do you plan to take?"

After Diane finished drawing blood, Heidi and I returned to the Guest House. The following day we sat around the lobby and looked through the bone marrow transplant "scrapbook." Actually, there are five albums filled with thank-you notes, cards and photos from guests. I was amazed at how many people who had stayed at the Guest House during their treatment had written to express their appreciation to Tom and Judy.

That Sunday evening Mom and Dad flew into Little Rock— they had stayed in Pennsylvania to celebrate Ashley's birthday at Tammy and Tim's— and we went out to eat together. Heidi and I were very candid in sharing our feelings of discouragement with my folks. None of us had much of an appetite that night. When we returned to the Guest House, we showed Mom and Dad the loose-leaf notebooks on the coffee table in the lobby, and they began looking through the accounts and testimonies of patients who had undergone bone marrow transplants. Later Mom wrote in her diary how these had bolstered her feelings at a low time. I took some of the books up to my room and sat up much of Sunday night reading about these patients and the encouragement they had to offer. The next morning, Monday, we had coffee and donuts about 7:30, then boarded a shuttle bus to the Arkansas Cancer Research Center.

The ACRC was founded by two physicians, Dr. Sundar Jagannath and Dr. Bart Barlogie, who were originally from the M.D. Anderson facility in Houston, Texas. Interestingly, they had come to Little Rock to set up this clinic at the invitation of Sam Walton. When we reached the hospital we met Sally, Dr. Barlogie's nurse. Heidi and I had both spoken to her several times by telephone prior to the appointment. She's a lot like Diane— kind and upbeat, just the type of person we needed at a time like this.

Sally directed us to follow signs leading to the bone marrow drawing center. The four of us sat down to wait in a room with a number of other patients. This was to be the first of many "draws" I would get in this department. Some of the veterans who were waiting with us said, "You'll be better off if you get 'Bone Marrow Bob'— he's really slick at the procedure." But I didn't get him.

After my first bone marrow draw, I had an EKG test and a chest X ray, followed by pulmonary tests to check the blood oxygen content in my arteries. These tests were long and exhausting, especially since I was still experiencing some pain in my rib cage. During this time, Heidi and my parents had to sit and wait, which they did a lot while in Arkansas. Waiting isn't easy, but God can use it to teach us many lessons, especially patience and trust.

When I explained my symptoms to Sally, she conferred with Dr. Jagannath. I wanted to take something for the pain in my rib cage, but he wouldn't give me anything stronger than Advil until they had the test results back. I did learn that the X rays they took showed a collection of fluid in my left lobe.

At about 2:00 P.M. I went over to the MRI building for another MRI scan. I was informed that I would be inside the MRI machine between four and five hours! They wanted to do a complete scan to check for any tumor activity. Naturally, the motive behind such an extensive test bothered me more than the test itself. After hearing how long the test would take, I suggested that Mom, Dad and Heidi go shopping to kill some time and return in four hours or so.

They drove to a nearby mall and just sat in the car crying and praying. Walking through the mall left them feeling like everything was meaningless and temporal. They certainly didn't feel like shopping. By the time they returned, I was almost finished.

As I came out of the MRI room, I was glad to see they were back, because I was hungry and wanted to go eat. Earlier that day we decided we were going to a special restaurant that served catfish, one of my favorite foods. In fact, while I was laying in that MRI tube, I kept my spirits up by thinking about the good catfish dinner I was going to eat when it was all over. My family was relieved to hear me express my hunger and enthusiasm to go do something fun.

The following morning we had our first appointment with Dr. Jagannath. It didn't take us long to discover he was a blunt, straightforward doctor. He had us pull our chairs up to his desk, and he used diagrams and charts to help us understand that we were dealing with a very serious disease, one that usually leads to death within three to five years. He didn't pull any punches. His facts were carefully documented and came from experience with a lot of patients. He told me flat out, "Chris, the usual age of diagnosis for this cancer is 67. You are only half that. Through standard chemotherapy you'll have about a year and a half to live.

"But we have two added options for you. First, we can give you a transplant using your own bone marrow. We'd like to try that route first.

"There's also a second option. You have four sisters. We can test them, and if you have a match and the transplant of your own marrow doesn't work, we can give you a transplant from one of them. We don't want to do that unless we have to, though, because it's a much more risky procedure."

After the meeting with Dr. Jagannath, the four of us were left alone in the room with a sheaf of papers of information about the treatment options and their possible side effects. It was heavy reading, but I needed to work through it because I had to sign a consent form for this new and experimental treatment to begin. Even though I felt like a guinea pig, I'm convinced there are times when the best thing to do is try an experimental treatment— and I did.

After I signed the forms, the doctor took me in for an examination, then showed me my chest and hip X rays. There were several lesions, or tumors, on my hips. The doctor advised me to keep life as normal as possible during treatment, and added, "Chris, if a bone breaks, we'll deal with it to heal it." He warned me not to carry any suitcases or anything else heavy for at least a year. *That's encouraging,* I thought. *It sounds like he expects me to be alive for at least another year.*

My next stop was Nuclear Medicine for a heart test, then a visit to surgery after lunch to have a catheter inserted into my chest in preparation for chemotherapy. As I came out of surgery after they inserted the catheter I thought, *This is the first step toward getting well.* I still felt a lot of fear, but I felt hopeful too. I gave Heidi and my parents a "thumbs up" as they wheeled me into X ray to be sure the catheter had been inserted in the proper position in my main artery.

I was on my way to recovery, I thought. The next step was chemotherapy. My treatment at the Arkansas Cancer Research Center was underway.

Chapter 10

Chemotherapy

For some people, the best option for dealing with cancer may be right across town— a local facility that provides excellent care. Others may choose an internationally respected facility such as M.D. Anderson in Houston, the Mayo Clinic in Rochester, Minnesota, Oschner's in New Orleans or Memorial Sloan-Kettering Cancer Center in New York.

For me, the best option was the Arkansas Cancer Research Center. According to Dr. Joshua Epstein, associate professor of medicine at the University of Arkansas in Little Rock, the division of hematology and oncology at ACRC has chosen to concentrate on multiple myeloma. Like all other cancers, multiple myeloma is a clonal disease. In other words, all the tumor cells originate from a single cell, which is referred to as the tumor stem cell. When cancer occurs, changes in the genetic material of the stem cell make it and the cells that grow from it unresponsive to the normal mechanisms God has designed to regulate the growth and development of tissue. This is consistent with the way all cancers develop. According to what I've read, myeloma tumor cells are the most mature "B cells" or lymphocytes that originate in the bone marrow. Their normal function is to produce immunoglobins, the antibodies that play a central role in the body's immune system.

Researchers have discovered that the cancerous cells in myeloma are not able to multiply. This has led to the hypothesis that a pool of immature, multiplying pretumor cells feeds into and causes the expansion of the tumor cell population.

The research conducted at the ACRC has included doctors from China, France, Italy and Japan as well as the United States. These studies, which have been carried out in collaboration with the National Institutes of Health, have focused on looking for ways to cause the patient's immune system to interrupt the development of myeloma from the pre-cancerous cells. Additional research has focused on increasing the effectiveness of chemotherapy through nutritional conditioning and minimizing resistance to drugs.

Modern medicine has developed three primary weapons to treat cancer, although others are in the works. These are surgery, chemotherapy and radiotherapy. Before the appropriate weapon or weapons are chosen for anyone's treatment, the medical team must make sure of the specific classification or grade of cancer, to what degree it has spread, and other factors.

Of course, the goal of cancer treatment is to get rid of all the cancer cells in a patient's body. One basic approach is to simply cut away the cancerous tissue— that's usually done through surgery. A second is to kill the cancer cells in the body. Radiation therapy, chemotherapy and immunotherapy are the primary tools for achieving this. The specific choices for any patient depend on the exact diagnosis, the stage of the cancer involved and the general health of the patient.

Although a bone marrow transplant loomed in my future, the next step for me was chemotherapy. As the term suggests, chemotherapy involves the use of chemicals to treat a disease. I guess you could say that any use of chemical medicines— pain killers, antibiotics, or others— could be called chemotherapy. However, in oncology or cancer treatment the term *chemotherapy* specifically refers to the use of chemicals that kill cancer cells.

Before I began chemo, Heidi and I, along with my parents, viewed a video to help acquaint us with the procedure and explain how the chemicals would be administered. The nurse showed Heidi and my parents how to administer the drugs into my catheter and how to keep it clean. I would be given four vials that would take approximately 24 hours to enter my bloodstream, and during that time I would swallow ten pills. This was extremely hard for me because I've always been used to taking care of myself and keeping my body in good shape. Now I would be inserting deadly chemicals into my body.

I know some people have the idea that chemotherapy is a last resort, used only when things are hopeless. However, my physicians were quick to assure me this really isn't the case.

Nor are side effects a major issue. Some people think chemotherapy doesn't work unless it makes you terribly ill. How sick the patient becomes depends on a number of factors, including the specific chemical used and the tolerance of the individual. Generally, any chemo patient can expect some unpleasant side effects. The main reason, as one oncologist explained it, is the chemical is actually poisoning you to help kill any left-over cancer cells.

I'll never forget what happened at 4:00 P.M. on April 14. This was when my first chemotherapy treatment began. At that moment the first drug entered my body to begin killing the disease. We left the department with a prayer on our hearts and our lips: "Lord, please use this treatment to wipe out every last cancer cell."

The following morning we met with Diane again to learn about changing my dressing and flushing my catheter. She was such a cheerful nurse and really knew her stuff. She used a dummy— she called him Chester— to demonstrate what she was doing, then carried out the procedures on me. Afterward she took us up to the second floor library to show us all the materials and papers describing the various treatment programs. At this point all four of us were feeling pretty low, but again we saw how gracious the Lord had been to put people like Diane in our paths to encourage us at those low points.

When we returned to the chemo room on the first floor, we met some of the other patients. Our spirits were lifted when we saw how healthy some of them looked. One patient told me, "Chris, you look so healthy. It's unbelievable." As I talked with him, I discovered that he lived just a short distance from the hospital and hadn't even known of the treatment available here. His cancer had progressed to the point where he had become bedfast by the time he arrived at the ACRC. Thankfully, he had experienced significant improvement since his treatment had begun.

The following day the alarm clock jarred us awake at 5:30 A.M.— it was time to head home from our first trip to the Arkansas Cancer Research Center. We boarded a USAir jet in Little Rock at 7:40 A.M. to fly to Charlotte, then on to Harrisburg. Traveling as a chemotherapy patient was a new experience for me— the medications have to be refrigerated if the trip is too long. During the flight I read Dave Dravecky's book, *Comeback*, which describes his return to baseball after he was diagnosed with cancer. He had faced many of the same questions I had been wrestling with, and as I read his book, it seemed that with each turn of the page I was feeling the same feelings he had felt.

Dave's story lifted my spirits. As we flew into Harrisburg, I told my parents and Heidi, "There are obstacles in the path— but they are not insurmountable."

Chapter 11

Clots, Complications and Hair Loss

Just a month and a half after we returned home to Pennsylvania, I began having complications with my lungs. I was fighting a great deal of fatigue and pain and had trouble breathing. One day I went home from the office and could barely walk up the steps to the house. When we discovered I had a fever, Heidi called the physicians at Little Rock, who suggested we check with my local doctor.

My biggest concern now was that this would somehow prevent me from being a candidate for a bone marrow transplant. We talked with the doctors in Little Rock, and they explained that I could still have the transplant, but they wanted to see me at the ACRC as soon as possible.

Dr. Weston ordered an X ray called a VQ scan, which showed I had blood clots in the lung, so he sent me to the Evangelical Hospital in Lewisburg. The pulmonary tests I was given the following day located several clots in my lung. The main clot was in a dangerous location— it was threatening to break loose and go straight to my heart at any time. Dr. William French, an interventional radiologist, had the task of inserting a screen above where they had located the clot. It was a very tedious job because the screen itself had to be inserted through the vein to protect my heart from the blood clot. If the clot loosened and entered my heart, I would die instantly!

Amazingly, I was allowed to remain awake for this delicate procedure, which was carried out under local anesthesia. I watched on a television screen located beside the bed, which the doctors also viewed as the operation proceeded. During those six hours, Dr. French and the other team members were candid with me about how serious things were. They also explained what they would do with the emergency equipment that was standing by in case the procedure failed.

I felt like I was watching a high-drama surgery, and I realized the risk was mine. This was not television or a movie, but real life! Several times I asked Dr. French, "Are you past the clot yet?" I felt incredible relief when he finally answered, "Yes, I am."

A few days later my parents and Heidi were present when Dr. French stopped by to see me in the hospital room. God had used him to spare me from an immediate life-threatening situation. During our post-operative conversation, we discovered that Dr. French had come to our local community hospital in 1991, only nine months before I needed his services. He specialized in non-surgical treatment of diseased arteries— in other words, things like using screens and medication to dissolve clots. He was one of only 2,000 doctors in the country who were qualified to do such procedures. We felt the Lord had placed him in our tiny hospital just for me— another evidence of His presence and care!

During this stay in the hospital in Lewisburg, I began to suffer a great deal of pain in my hip. An X ray showed nothing, so Dr. Weston and Dr. French conferred and concluded that the pain was a result of the procedure of inserting the screen to protect me from the blood clot. As I was able to move around, the pain lessened, and I was thankful for that relief, although my fever persisted.

Looking back now, I realize that this was one of my lowest points during the illness. After the hope of a transplant, I had felt somewhat optimistic. But this sudden bout with pulmonary emboli was disheartening.

I began to feel like the cancer had damaged my body to the extent that I had no hope of recovery. The doctors tried to reassure me that this wasn't the case and that I still was a good candidate for a transplant. But I was extremely weak and felt utterly helpless.

That Sunday morning, with all my family at church, I lay in my hospital bed feeling alone and depressed. I cried out to God to give me some encouragement. Later I learned that this particular morning Heidi was also feeling really low as she took our girls to Sunday school and church. When she walked into our Sunday school class, everyone started bombarding her with questions about my condition. She finally broke down and told the class how discouraged she was. Tearfully she exclaimed, "We are at a low point, and we really need you guys right now." Our class responded by taking that entire class period to pray for Heidi, me and our family.

I didn't know about their prayer time, but while I lay in that hospital bed crying out for the Lord to speak to me, I heard a knock on my door. A dark-haired, bearded man asked, "Are you Chris Bingaman?" He introduced himself. "I am Dominique Herbst." I had heard of Dominique through my father, but had never met him before.

His next words took my by surprise. "Chris, I was in Sunday school when they requested prayer for you. During the prayer time the Lord just really impressed me to leave class early and come and see you. As I left church I told my wife I needed to go see Chris Bingaman now." That man's response to God's prompting was the answer to my prayer! God used that experience to reassure me once again of His presence.

It also reminded me of the importance of being sensitive to God's Spirit. Dominique's willingness to immediately respond to the Spirit's prompting has challenged me to become more aware of the Lord's leading in my own life.

I learned another valuable lesson at that time, through the pain in my hip. My mother and three other women from our church had become my personal prayer warriors in response to the pain in my hip. These four women covenanted together to pray specifically that I would get relief from this pain. During my hospital stay my hip pain did lessen, although on the trip home it returned. As I walked into the house, I felt extreme discomfort. Unknown to me, Mom called her "group" and they began to specifically pray about the pain.

Later that day the pain went away, and it never returned! At this point in my journey, that was a real witness to answered prayer, and it especially taught me the value of praying specifically. I believe the Lord delights in using the answer to our prayers to make His presence known. However, we need to be specific in our requests. When we are, it helps us focus on His presence and His answers to those requests.

The next day, Monday, was special. Three of my sisters, Tammy, Lori and Mary Beth, stopped by to see me. But that wasn't the only reason they had come to the hospital; they were on a vital medical mission. They had come for blood tests to determine which of them might qualify to donate bone marrow that matched mine in case I needed a donor in the future. My other sister, Heidi, who lived in Montana at the time, was being tested there. Tammy, Lori, Mary Beth, my wife and my parents all formed a circle in the hallway, with arms around each other, and thanked God for watching over me, then asked for strength and direction for the future.

On May 15 I was able to come home from the hospital. During dinner that evening, we received a call from Dr. Barlogie's nurse. He wanted to see me in Arkansas May 26-27 for further testing before starting the next round of chemotherapy. It was discouraging to realize I needed to make the trip again so quickly, but the nurse explained that they wanted to be sure about some factors that may have developed because of the surgery for the blood clot.

On Memorial Day, Heidi and I flew back to Little Rock as my sister Mary Beth kept our girls. The following day, Tuesday, we both felt discouraged as we waited for test results that were being shipped overnight from the Lewisburg hospital to be compared with the tests I had been given in Arkansas. We were alerted that the doctors might have to make a surgical incision to get a piece of lung for testing, but they finally decided that wasn't necessary. What a relief!

After they started me on another round of chemo, I was able to return to Pennsylvania. The bone marrow tests they took revealed that the rate of cancer in the marrow remained unchanged in spite of the first round of chemotherapy. The exact number was 45 percent, identical to my original test.

On Friday, May 29, we were all expecting results from the blood tests to see who might match. Heidi answered the phone when it rang, and she, Tammy and Mary Beth were with Mom. They came over to the office together to share the news. They walked into my office together—I was surprised to see them. Heidi walked over to me, threw her arms around me and said, "Chris, meet your two matches." Either Tammy or Mary Beth would be able to provide marrow for a transplant. It was a time of incredible joy, mixed with many tears of thankfulness.

I had been meditating on several key verses during this time. One of them was Jeremiah 29:11:

> *"For I know the plans I have for you," declares the Lord, "plans to prosper you and not to harm you, plans to give you hope and a future."*

As I kept praying and crying out to the Lord for healing, I sensed a greater closeness to Him. Even though I was still fearful, I felt the chemotherapy was beginning to take effect. In fact, in just a matter of a few weeks I was able to run again! It was only from my home to my parents' house—a far shorter distance than usual—but I shed tears of joy over the fact that I was making progress.

A couple of months later we headed back to Arkansas for the third time. While we were away, the Shaffer family cared for Emily and Lindsey, our two oldest. Scott and Cathy Shaffer not only gave up their bed for our daughters but also supervised the girls' school assignments, since their sons Nathan and Andrew were in the same classes as our girls. Leah stayed with Mom and Dad, while Tammy kept Audrey. This four-and-a-half week trip proved to be especially difficult, so it was particularly helpful to have close friends and a big family to help keep things together.

The plan during this time was to harvest my bone marrow to use in what's known as an autologous transplant—a transplant of my own marrow. However, the initial blood tests held bad news. My cancer rate had dropped slightly, to 40 percent. I'd been hoping for greater progress as a result of the chemotherapy, but at least there was some progress.

Heidi and I met with Dr. David Vesole and two transplant nurses. I would be hospitalized at the University of Arkansas Hospital for three nights and given Cytoxin, one of the strongest chemotherapy drugs in use. They would give me shots in the stomach to raise my blood count, and they warned me of possible side effects— chills, fever, diarrhea and vomiting.

Dr. Vesole explained that the donor of preference if I needed one would be a brother, but that a sister would be next best. I was somewhat surprised that he brought this up, since this was the first time we had seriously discussed the possibility of my receiving a donor transplant. Mary Beth would be preferable to Tammy since she had never been pregnant. Apparently, having children builds up certain antigens in the blood that can lead to rejection. Dr. Vesole told me he had performed 35 donor transplants. At this point we were simply gathering information. We had no idea I would actually have to go through with this life-threatening treatment.

Two days later they began harvesting stem cells from my body. They also gave me a platelet transfusion. I was amazed at how easily these procedures were carried out. But Heidi and I began noticing something else— my hair had started falling out!

I recall walking into the bathroom one morning, taking a washcloth and rubbing it across my head. Clumps of hair just fell out. I thought for the first time, *I really look sick now. I look just like a cancer patient.* That bothered me almost as much as any of the infections or other medical problems. Within a week my head was as smooth as a cue ball, and I began suffering chest pains and fever.

It took four days to harvest all the stem cells that were needed from my bone marrow. The following day we flew home. Heidi and I had been away from our children for more than a month. It was the first time we had been away from the kids for that long— another difficult and painful part of this ordeal.

A month later we returned to Arkansas—my fourth trip—to have the cells transplanted that had been harvested from my bone marrow. When they checked my marrow count, the results were not good; the cancer count was still at 23 percent. Again we stayed at the familiar Guest House, and I was given the transplant on an outpatient basis.

My first bone marrow transplant coincided with election day 1992, an especially memorable night in Little Rock. Arkansas governor Bill Clinton was elected president. I heared sirens and saw a lot of activity that night as Mr. Clinton prepared to give his victory speech at the old Arkansas State House, which was located in downtown Little Rock not far from where we were staying. One of my most vivid memories is lying in bed listening to the sounds of celebration and wondering if I would still be alive to witness another election four years later.

The harvest procedure itself was done on an outpatient basis—I was one of the first at ACRC to try this. The doctors began my chemotherapy at the clinic, and I would take an IV pump in a bag back to my room every night. I felt so sick after receiving the transplant—at times so sick they considered admitting me to the hospital.

Not only was I too sick to eat, I couldn't even stand the smell of food. Heidi had to give me an injection of GMCSF, a stimulating drug for the new bone marrow, every night. I frequently felt a terrible pain in my chest, and at times I would throw up hours after receiving the injection.

About eight days after the transplant took place, I began feeling better. First, my appetite returned, then I felt like walking again, a nice change from days of lying in bed.

During the almost four weeks I was in Little Rock, Heidi and I met a nurse named Tim Fix. We are sure the Lord arranged for us to meet him at the ACRC during my treatment there. Tim became a major source of encouragement, and because of his knowledge of the program, he often supplied us with information about what was happening and helped us know what to expect. We also were able to get together with him a number of times socially. Tim and his family added a lot of cheer to our lengthy stay in Arkansas.

Finally, it was time for me to return home— and keep waiting.

By January, almost a year after my initial cancer diagnosis, I returned to Arkansas for another check on progress. We hoped the cancer would be gone, but it was not. The bone marrow test showed a cancer count of .04. Despite the newly treated marrow, some cancer still remained. The results were promising, but not good enough.

The original plan was for me to undergo another autologous transplant, using my own bone marrow. Now the doctors told me they didn't think this was the best approach. They felt I needed the donor transplant, which would be more risky. I would need to spend 35 days in the hospital in isolation and would be forced to stay in Arkansas approximately 150 days.

We boarded our plane for Pennsylvania with grieving hearts. Leaving our girls again for this length of time was painful for Heidi and me, but it seemed like the only way to save my life. "The Lord knows we have these girls to care for, and if this is the path He's laid out for us, I'm sure He'll find a way for their care," Heidi said to me.

That night we stayed at my parents' house because the girls were already there. We sat up talking with Mom and Dad until the wee hours of the morning. Heidi explained that she had felt all along it would take a donor transplant. She was so encouraging to me, even though all this was disrupting her life as well.

Though our hearts were heavy because none of the previous treatments— the chemotherapy or the transplant of my own bone marrow— had eliminated the cancer, we knew that whatever lay ahead, the Lord was with us. After all, He had promised His presence. At that point we didn't realize that the Lord would use one individual to provide for the two biggest needs— my bone marrow and the care of our four girls. That person was my sister Mary Beth.

Chapter 12

Mary Beth

Back when I was in high school and my sister Mary Beth was a little girl, she attended every basketball game I played. She sat with the cheerleaders and cheered for me, and when I went to college, my parents tell me she used to walk around the house hugging my picture and crying and talking about how much she missed me.

One special occasion stands out in my memory. Our soccer team from Messiah College was playing against Bucknell, close to where my family lives. After the game, which ended in a tie, my family joined me on the field for a few minutes before the team headed back to the locker room. Clutching a bag of candy, Mary Beth ran up to me and hugged my leg. As she gripped my leg and handed me the candy, I realized how special our relationship was.

Mary Beth is petite with brown hair and eyes. And she's full of life. She has a wonderful sense of humor. In fact, my parents say she's the most like me of my four sisters. Mom has always said we're two of a kind.

When I returned to Pennsylvania from Little Rock, after the doctors had told me I'd need a transplant, I began to get sick. By Friday evening, I realized I was probably in the middle of another bout with pneumonia. Heidi took me to the hospital and I was admitted. Mary Beth, who was attending Messiah College at the time, was home on vacation. Since we had to leave suddenly to go to the hospital, she came over to stay with our children.

On Saturday afternoon Mary Beth came to the hospital for a visit. By that time I was feeling much better, so we ate pizza and played games in the room. It was a great time of fellowship. In fact, that evening she stayed in my room, sleeping in a chair. The next morning as she was preparing to leave, she told me, "Chris, the Lord's laid it on my heart to take off my last semester of school. I'm seriously thinking about keeping your kids while you have the transplant."

"Mary Beth, that's a nice thought. I really think that's great, but I could never let you do that."

But Mary Beth is a lot like some other people in our family— more than a little persistent. "Chris, I'm telling you I'm praying about this. The Lord has laid it on my heart."

The next day, Monday, Mary Beth left to go back to Messiah, wondering if she would be able to postpone her student teaching. That same day she talked with her education supervisor, who told her, "Mary Beth, you are already in the curriculum program. You can come back the following fall to do your student teaching." That confirmed for her that she was making the right decision. She called my dad and told him what she had decided, and that she knew her choice was from the Lord.

The following day, Tuesday, I received a phone call at the hospital. "Chris, it's Mary Beth. I'm just calling to let you know I've talked to my advisors down here and everyone at school. My decision is made. I'm taking off my last semester. I'm going to take care of your girls when you go for the transplant." The Lord had been working on me, and I readily accepted her offer.

I lay in the hospital bed shaking my head and thinking, *This is incredible. Clearly this must be of the Lord.* Then Mary Beth added, "You know, Chris, I never would have thought about this if you hadn't come down with pneumonia."

How wise God was to use my infirmity to work things out so Heidi and I would have the best possible person to take care of our girls. Once again, my suffering had a purpose. And once again I was made aware that, just as He promised, He was with me. He had every detail worked out well in advance. There were no surprises to Him, no loose ends left untied.

At first I didn't realize how strongly Mary Beth felt the Lord wanted her to do this. I thought she was just making the offer because she loved me. As I talked with her, however, I could sense the relief that she felt in doing what she knew God had called her to do. She kept telling me, "Chris, you just don't know how much peace I have about doing this."

Later on I learned the rest of the story. A few weeks before, she and Dad had talked. She told me he had said, "Mary Beth, we really need to find someone to help Chris and Heidi with their girls. They'll have to be gone three and a half months for this transplant." She assured me, and I know it's true, Dad had no intention of trying to make her feel like she should do it. But she sensed that God might be tapping her on the shoulder, and she said, "Daddy, I should be the one."

Dad told her then the same thing I told her later at the hospital. "Mary Beth, that's a wonderful offer to make, but there's no way."

After her visit with me on that Saturday, Mary Beth spent Sunday evening contemplating all the things she wanted to do— graduate from school, spend time with her roommates, get started with her teaching career. Then she began thinking about our girls and how important it would be for them not to be separated. Her friend Jennifer helped her sort her thoughts out. She cried and prayed. During the night she woke up, pulled out her Bible and began reading in Philippians. She wanted to know, "Lord, is this desire from You? I really want to know Your will." Then she read Philippians 2:13: "For it is God who works in you to will and to act according to his good purpose."

Later when she talked with my parents, Dad reminded her, "Mary Beth, for a decision this big, no one else can make it for you. You have to make the choice yourself."

Mary Beth made some big sacrifices. She dropped out of school to keep our kids. She gave her bone marrow for my transplant. But God looked out for her during her semester off. She had become discouraged about her dating life— in fact, she had told us how she hadn't been happy with the guy she was currently dating. Just to show you how the Lord works and how obedience brings blessing, while she was keeping our kids she met Steve Will, who is now her husband.

Steve was in the middle of changing jobs when he learned about my ordeal with cancer. He had heard the story about how Mary Beth was keeping our girls and wrote her a letter to commend her for what she was doing.

A local Christian radio station was sponsoring a social at a roller skating rink. Mary Beth took our children there to skate, and Steve, who was home for a week, came to the rink, saw this girl skate by and thought, *Man, who's that?* When he found out it was Mary Beth and how much she had grown up since he had seen her last, they began to talk.

You know how one thing leads to another. Steve began to come by to see her—just to help with the kids, of course.

That's yet another of the evidences of God fulfilling His promise to be with us. He put it on my sister's heart to keep our girls—not to mention her willingness to give me her bone marrow. Then He gave her the blessing of a husband.

Chapter 13

A Life-saving Transplant

Tuesday, March 2, 1993, was a day we both anticipated and dreaded. We were scheduled to leave that day for the BMT, as we came to refer to the bone marrow transplant procedure. So we said a tearful good-bye to our girls and extended family and began our journey into uncharted waters. The weather was typical of March, cold and windy with a mixture of clouds and sun. We would likely be away for three to three-and-a-half months. One of the hardest things for me was leaving and wondering if I would ever drive up my driveway to my home and family again.

An estimated 16,000 children and adults are stricken every year with some form of serious blood-related disease. The only hope for survival for many of them is a marrow transplant. Nearly 70 percent of those individuals are unable to find a suitable match within their families. Their chances of finding an unrelated match lie somewhere between one in a hundred and one in a million!

Mary Beth and Tammy had done some research on the subject of a match. They found it defined as "a person or thing that's exactly like another in one or more specified qualities." At a celebration dinner on March 16, 1994, one year after my transplant, the two of them stood before 100 guests who had gathered with us to celebrate and give thanks. They described several different kinds of matches, like socks, shoes, and gloves. Then they presented me with a large basket filled with matches of every kind—kitchen matches, book matches, even fireplace matches. It was a lighthearted moment, but it commemorated a very serious situation.

The doctors told us it was extremely rare for three out of five siblings to match exactly. The chances of a sibling match are only 1 in 4, while the chance of such matches outside the family are only 1 in 200,000. Maybe that's why Tammy and Mary Beth, whose bone marrow matched mine, decided to give me that basket labeled "a lifetime supply of matches."

During that same special evening the girls read the three verses from Proverbs 3 that had come to mean so much to me and to all of us:

> *Trust in the Lord with all your heart, and lean not on your own understanding; in all your ways acknowledge him, and he will make your paths straight. Do not be wise in your own eyes; fear the Lord and shun evil. This will bring health to your body and [marrow] to your bones (vv. 5-8).*

If anybody can relate to the concept of health to the body and marrow to the bones, I can!

As the doctors explained to all of us, Mary Beth's marrow would be taken by means of an outpatient procedure. There would be no risk to her, although they did have some trouble finding a vein in her arm when they gave her an IV. She said she didn't feel any pain even then.

The plan was for me to undergo a transplant from Mary Beth. I would then spend 35 days in the hospital in Little Rock in isolation, and a total of almost 150 days in Arkansas undergoing extensive treatment.

The reason for my extended hospital stay was that my immune system would be destroyed by chemotherapy treatment in order to prepare me for the transplant of the new marrow. To protect against infection I would be confined in isolation until Mary Beth's marrow grafts and her immunities took over my body.

My wife had been in much prayer about our March 2 departure for Arkansas. She asked God to give her something to cling to, something to help us take that big first step away from home towards our hope of restoration. As He had many times before, God gave her a promise of His presence and hope for the upcoming days. It came from the Book of Joshua, chapter 1, particularly verses 8 and 9.

Meditate on [God's Word] day and night, so that you may be careful to do everything written in it. Then you will be prosperous and successful. . . . Be strong and courageous. Do not be terrified; do not be discouraged, for the Lord your God will be with you wherever you go.

Then God gave Heidi a remarkable word picture from Joshua 3. This chapter tells about Joshua leading the people of Israel out of the wilderness to the banks of the Jordan River. He was about to lead them across the river into the Promised Land. The river was at flood stage, and the priests were carrying the Ark of the Covenant. As soon as the priests set foot into the water, the waters flowing downstream would be cut off and stand like a wall, and the people would walk across on dry land. This is exactly what happened as Joshua 3:15-16 records.

As Heidi explained the analogy to me, we could compare our journey through this bone marrow transplant to the Israelites crossing the Jordan River. We couldn't cross the river until we got our feet wet. That meant walking out our door, getting into our car, and traveling to Arkansas. Only then would God begin to part the waters and provide the way to the other side, the hoped-for restoration of my health, our "promised land."

We arrived in Little Rock on Tuesday, and I underwent extensive testing on Wednesday and Thursday. Friday we had our final meeting with Dr. Luther Glenn before I was admitted to the hospital. It proved to be one of the most discouraging meetings we had. The usually optimistic Dr. Glenn chose not to give us a hearty pep talk.

"Chris, there's a thirty percent chance of death through this procedure," he explained. "Fifty percent of the people who have this transplant are able to resume a reasonably normal life, but you will have to stay here for three to four months." Then he added, "You're in good health. You have a good match, and I'm confident. But you need to know the risks involved. And I have to be honest with you about them."

As Heidi and I walked back to the Guest House Inn, our hearts were heavy, and the next morning we both felt solemn. When we turned to God's Word for comfort, He did not leave us comfortless. He reminded me of the first nine verses of Psalm 116, a precious passage given me by another cancer survivor, Marianne Owen, not long after my diagnosis.

> *I love the Lord, for He heard my voice; he heard my cry for mercy. Because he turned his ear to me, I will call on him as long as I live. The cords of death entangled me, the anguish of the grave came upon me; I was overcome by trouble and sorrow. Then I called on the name of the Lord: "O Lord, save me!" The Lord is gracious and righteous; our God is full of compassion. The Lord protects the simplehearted; when I was in great need, he saved me. Be at rest once more, O my soul, for the Lord has been good to you. For You, O Lord, have delivered my soul from death, my eyes from tears, my feet from stumbling, that I may walk before the Lord in the land of the living.*

These words of hope gave us additional courage to move forward. Heidi and I decided to go out for lunch. As we walked through the lobby, we spotted a dear friend we had met on an earlier visit to Arkansas. Mr. and Mrs. Sigmund Etter were from Germany, and Sylvie was receiving treatment for the same type of cancer as mine. We excitedly approached Mr. Etter, who was sitting in the lobby alone. When we asked how his wife was doing, we were shocked to hear that she had just died and they were preparing for her burial. It was devastating news as we neared my transplant date.

On Sunday we drove to a local church we had attended during our previous time in Little Rock. The Cornerstone Bible Fellowship Church, its pastor Jim Ehrhard and its people were another of God's provisions to us during this dark time. The pastor's wife, Debbie, had undergone a BMT for breast cancer, so they were familiar with what we were facing. It was while attending Cornerstone that I met a fellow named Steve Arnold, who was originally from a town just 15 minutes from my hometown. Steve and his family ministered to us with regular visits to the hospital, meals and, most of all, intercessory prayer. Many of the members from Cornerstone came to donate platelets for me following the transplant.

After eating lunch with some church members, Heidi and I drove into downtown Little Rock and decided to walk around. Since it was Sunday, the streets were quiet. We were in a somber mood as we drank in the sunlight and inhaled the fresh air. In a few short hours, I would be admitted to the University Hospital, where I would remain on an isolated floor for 30 to 35 days. I desperately wanted to be assured that I would walk off that floor in a month and live to see the light of day.

We arrived at the hospital and were greeted by a lovely British nurse named Allison, ready to admit us. The entire wall to the left of my bed was glass, giving us a great view of the skyline of Little Rock. As I mentioned, Isaiah 40:31, which says that those who hope in the Lord will soar like eagles, had become very special to me. The night before I left for the transplant, two young boys, Nathan and Andrew Shaffer, the sons of our company controller, had presented me with a stuffed eagle with suction cups on its wings, which we immediately attached to the window wall. That toy was a visible reminder of the hope that God would not let us alone during the next few dark weeks.

I began a week of intense chemotherapy designed to destroy my immune system. Without a transplant, I would die. Heidi stayed with me in my room. At night she slept on a recliner chair, clad in a gown, mask, gloves and shoe coverings, which were required of everyone who entered the BMT floor.

My parents and Mary Beth were scheduled to fly down March 13, and the transplant was to be performed three days later. The marrow would be taken from Mary Beth's bones and given to me the same day.

Saturday, March 13, we called home and learned that the worst snowstorm of the year had hit. We realized that my parents and Mary Beth were unable to make their scheduled flight to Arkansas that day, and the next two days were filled with anxiety. Finally, after much prayer and an incredible series of events, they arrived in Little

Rock on Monday evening, the night before the transplant.

Later Dad filled me in on the details of their trip. He, Mom and Mary Beth were to fly out of Harrisburg Saturday morning. As they drove the 50-plus miles from Kreamer, the snow really began coming down. When they reached Harrisburg, they learned their flight had been canceled. Because I'd already been undergoing the chemotherapy, I had to have the transplant by Tuesday at the latest. Realizing the urgency of getting Mary Beth to Little Rock, Dad and Mom became quite concerned over the situation. By the time they had driven back to Kreamer, approximately six to eight inches of snow had fallen.

It snowed heavily the rest of the day; by the following morning 28 inches of snow blanketed the Pennsylvania landscape. It was a blizzard of historic proportions, still referred to as "the blizzard of '93," and all travel throughout the Northeast had been halted.

Sunday after dinner Dad phoned our travel agent at her home. She agreed to call and see what she could arrange. Forty-five minutes later she phoned back. "Can you get to Baltimore? There's a flight leaving there on Monday." Since it was more than twice as far away as Harrisburg, and all the roads were closed, Dad wasn't sure how, but he told her, "I have a four-wheel drive, and I'm willing to give it a try. The only problem is, with the roads closed, I'll probably get stopped by the National Guard."

"My father is a county commissioner," our travel agent replied. "I'll get him to call the National Guard and explain the situation."

Ten minutes later the travel agent phoned again. "Here's a name and number to call if you get stopped."

Mom, Dad and Mary Beth packed their Ford Bronco with extra gear, snow shovels and food. They finally left about 2:30 Sunday afternoon. The roads were terrible—one lane barely open on a four-lane highway, but at least they were moving toward Baltimore. When they reached the intersection where they were to take Interstate 83, they found huge piles of snow and a barricade that read "Road Closed." One other car sat near the intersection.

Everything else was deserted.

After waiting awhile, Dad got out of his Bronco and walked over to talk to the man in the other car. "Let's try old U.S. 15," the other man suggested. "Perhaps maybe they've plowed it." They drove over there and found it open and relatively free of snow. Within 15 miles they were able to get on Interstate 83 and drive into Baltimore by late that evening. There was only a foot of snow in the Baltimore area.

Monday morning they arrived at the Baltimore airport two hours ahead of their scheduled 7:00 A.M. flight time. The place was jammed! After they stood in line for over an hour, they heard an announcement they had been dreading. "Flight 55 to Charlotte, North Carolina, has been canceled. The plane is still in New England."

Dad rushed over to explain the urgency of the situation to the gate attendant, who promptly called her supervisor. He took them to another gate for a later flight. "I'm not sure I can get you on here—but it's the best I can do."

Unfortunately, they found that flight totally packed as well. There were absolutely no seats available. By this time Dad felt desperate.

But once again the Lord came through. The USAir attendant placed a phone call, then told Dad, "I have seats reserved for you on a flight to St. Louis. From there you'll be able to connect with TWA directly into Little Rock. I'll issue your tickets for both legs of the flight."

Dad felt as though an entire truckload of lumber had been lifted from his heart. If nothing else, St. Louis was less than an eight-hour drive from Little Rock. Once they landed there, he could rent a car and get Mary Beth to the hospital in time for Tuesday's transplant.

However, the flight from Baltimore to St. Louis also was delayed—the pilot couldn't get to the airport on time due to the snow—and they missed their connection with TWA in St. Louis by 10 minutes. Fortunately, another flight was scheduled to leave just two hours later. Finally, at 5:30 Monday afternoon, their plane touched down in Little Rock, and all three of them wept tears of happiness.

While Mary Beth, who had been caring for our daughters, was in Arkansas to give me her bone marrow, God provided child care once again. Heidi had good friends named Andy and Kendra Aucker. God prompted Kendra to offer to take a week's vacation and move her family (they have two little girls) into our home to care for our daughters until Mary Beth returned. Heidi's sister Tracy Spigelmyer and her husband, Craig, also joined them.

Before the transplant could take place, I had to undergo what was known as the hydration process for chemo. That involved four days of taking 150 pills per day. On two of the days I was given Cytoxin, one of the strongest chemicals used for chemotherapy. Monday was to be a day of rest, before the transplant on Tuesday. I tolerated the chemotherapy pretty well, though I was nauseated a good deal of the time and threw up several times.

March 16 became a watershed date in my life. Besides being my wife Heidi's birthday, it was the day I received a life-saving transplant of my sister's bone marrow.

Heidi stayed with Mary Beth as she was prepared for surgery. My wife later told me that Mary Beth felt a wonderful peace, with absolutely no anxiety about what was about to take place. She even fell asleep while she was waiting. It must have been that "peace that passes all understanding."

After Mary Beth was wheeled into the outpatient surgery center, Heidi joined Mom and Dad in my room as we waited for my new marrow. At approximately 1:30 that afternoon, my nurse, Nancy, announced that the marrow had arrived. It looked like two bags of whole blood. The nurse placed it on my hospital table, and we all just stared at it. It was a sacred moment. Dad said, "We need to pray," and he led us in asking the Lord that this cancer-free marrow would bring complete restoration to his son.

Then the marrow was hooked up to an IV line and began flowing into my bloodstream. We were told that the marrow would find its way to the bone cavity. Amazing!

Over the next two weeks, the days passed slowly. Heidi spent each night sleeping in the recliner in my room, and we ate breakfast together each morning. She would walk back across to the Guest House to shower and pick up the mail. She usually returned around 5:00 p.m. to join me for supper and the rest of the evening.

During the days following the transplant, my blood counts were closely monitored. A nurse would come in every morning and write the count on the board. For days my counts continued to drop as the chemo took its effects. We eagerly were waiting for the day when the count would bottom out and begin to climb. That would mean that my new marrow had taken hold, or grafted, and I would have started the process of recovery to healthy life. That turn took place the morning of March 25. We were elated when my counts finally started to go up!

As I was having my devotions that morning, I asked Heidi about the passage in Joshua that had been so meaningful to her. I had not read it for myself, so I turned to it that morning. I was reading out of a modern translation called *The Way*. Chapter 4, verse 19, reads: "It was on the 25th of March that the Lord performed that miracle for them" [the miracle of crossing the Jordan]. I told Heidi, "Isn't that interesting! Today is March 25." Later that afternoon as I was showering, it was almost as if the Lord was speaking audibly to me, saying, "Chris, don't you see? This is the day that I am beginning that miracle in you." I had no certainty of what was ahead, but the Lord was once again using His Word to rekindle my hope.

Heidi wrote a wonderful letter to my parents just a week after the transplant. It read:

March 22, 1993

Dearest Max and Martha,

    It's 11:30 p.m. Chris is sleeping and persevering with a sore throat. He is still doing very well! Tomorrow morning I will go to give platelets. Chris will probably need platelets. Today the nurses told me they fight over who will get to take care of

Chris. He has a new pair of pjs on. He looks great. He thinks his hair is beginning to come out again. I tell him that he has literally given his body as a living sacrifice to the Lord.

I just had to tell you how delightful it was to have you both here. It was a big week. I'm glad you could be here to share it. Also it was very nice for me to have a couple of days of someone caring for me. Don't get me wrong. I'm doing fine and I'm ready, willing and glad to persevere here. It was very refreshing to have someone take me out to eat, drive me places and just take care of me. It was especially so after the strenuous week we had of tests and doctor visits [prior to the transplant] . . . as usual, it was perfect timing. On Saturday when you left, Chris's white count went to 0.2. He's getting a little weaker and his throat is a little sore. It will be a difficult time for him to just get through this.

Mary Beth called. I miss her. She's unbelievable with the kids. How can we ever, ever repay her?!

Lonnie Gelnett called and gave us Psalm 20:1-5. Their family prays this for us. God took me to Psalm 21:1-6. It was exciting to read that His message to me is consistent!

I love you both dearly. Thank you for your unbelievable and unending support. I am getting tired, better go to bed.

Love,

Heidi

The Scripture verse Lonnie gave us fit my situation to a tee, and I felt it was especially appropriate since he is a former cancer patient. The Lord had answered us in our distress. The name of the God of Jacob had protected me, and He had sent me help from the sanctuary and strengthened me! Looking back, I see how He granted me according to our hearts' desire and fulfilled His purpose.

That's why we've been able to rejoice in His salvation and "lift up our banners in the name of our God." He has truly fulfilled all our petitions without question. His presence has been with us!

Despite being plagued with nausea and a sore throat, I felt relatively good for the 35 days I spent on the transplant floor. I had no pain to speak of, and only once did I have a fever. However, the high doses of prednisone they gave me made me hyper. I couldn't seem to get to bed until after 11, and despite the sleeping pill I was given almost every night, I would still wake up at 4 or 5 A.M.

During this time I did a lot of reading and wrote quite a few notes to friends back in Pennsylvania. I also kept in touch with the office by phone, and tried to walk at least two miles each day on a treadmill in the sun room, which was just down the hallway on the transplant floor.

Two weeks after the transplant, Dr. Glenn came in and said that they needed to do a bone marrow draw to see what my marrow was doing. This surprised me, but we were told that it was a routine procedure. Later we realized that this aspiration was being taken exactly one year after I had my first bone marrow aspiration.

Two days later Dr. Glenn and Nancy, my nurse, entered the room. I could see that the expressions on their faces had changed. They chatted for a moment. Finally, Nancy said to the doctor, "Well, are you going to tell him?" Dr. Glenn proceeded to explain the results of my bone marrow aspiration. He said that the report was negative for any signs of cancer cells. The word *negative* had never sounded so good!

Our hearts were overwhelmed with joy as we sensed God's presence in that room in a special way. As we looked at the calendar, we realized that it was one year *to the day* that we had received the news that cancer had invaded my marrow. Now, a year later, I was again cancer-free. We truly had hope! The icing on the cake was that my parents were to arrive in Little Rock that night. We would be able to share this great news with them in person!

I finally reached the point where I was allowed to leave the hospital and take up residence at the Guest House while continuing my treatment on an outpatient basis. It just happened that I was discharged on Easter Sunday, an Easter I will never forget.

At the end of April, Mom, Dad and Mary Beth made arrangements to bring our four daughters to Arkansas to visit us. It was a fantastic reunion! We were so thankful that God had protected them during our separation.

During May and early June, as I walked back and forth to the clinic for treatments, I would watch planes flying overhead, and I dreamed of the day Heidi and I would board one to fly back to Pennsylvania. That day finally arrived in mid-June, and we were met at the Harrisburg Airport by four extremely excited girls who were waiting with their family for their mom and dad. But those girls weren't nearly as excited as we were.

After my return to Pennsylvania, I began to experience the typical battles of a weak immune system. At first I felt reasonably well, but as the doctors lowered my dosage of prednisone, I felt exhausted. At times I couldn't even walk up a flight of stairs.

I also continued to battle nausea throughout the fall and winter. I had to almost force myself to eat, since no food tasted or smelled very good.

But my biggest challenge was fighting off a virus called CMV. Several times I was required to return to Arkansas because this virus kept showing up in my blood. One time it even turned up in my lungs. Whenever this virus occurred I was forced to take doses of a strong intravenous antibiotic, which made my stomach problems even worse.

That winter I began feeling depressed. The doctors had warned us this could happen as a reaction to my being taken off all the drugs, especially the prednisone. I kept coming into the office and trying to work every day, but many days I would just sit in my chair and want to be left alone.

Yet despite the bouts with depression, nausea and other factors, I knew the Lord was with me, and I was grateful for the victory over cancer and the continued assurance of His presence.

My parents' Christmas letter that year put it so well:

Dear Family and Friends,

At this special time of year, we want our family to join in wishing you and your family a wonderful holiday season as we celebrate the coming of our Savior. . . . Many of you might want an update on Chris. The following passage in Isaiah 40:30 describes his condition almost two years ago, "Even the youth shall faint and grow weary and the young man shall utterly fall."

During this period . . . Isaiah 40:31 became his hope and strength. "But those who wait on the Lord shall renew their strength. They shall mount up with wings like eagles, they shall run and not be weary, and they shall walk and not faint." We rejoice and praise God that Chris is able to run and walk again and is enjoying almost complete health.

Chris had three bone marrow biopsies since the transplant March 16, which have all returned showing no signs of cancer. Further test results have indicated all of Chris's marrow and blood type are those of Mary Beth, his sister, the donor.

We all knew from the beginning of my illness that if I was to be made whole again, it would only be by the grace and mercy of the Lord. We all felt thankful beyond words for His intervention, and for the way He used the medical knowledge He had given the doctors who performed a perfect transplant.

Chapter 14

Spiritual Battles and Lessons

Probably the most important lesson I learned from my ordeal is reflected in the title we chose for this book— *The Promise of God's Presence.* The Lord walked with me every step of the way. Of that I'm absolutely sure.

The second most important lesson I learned is don't ever give up. It's always too soon to quit.

Someone gave me a cartoon that depicts a pelican swallowing a frog. Maybe you've seen it. I smile every time I look at it. The frog's head and most of his body are inside the pelican's beak; only his legs and front arms are dangling outside. But that frog hasn't surrendered. In fact, with his front arms he's doing a pretty good job of choking the bird that's trying to swallow him!

But I don't want you to get the idea that I never felt like giving up. To be candid, it was a battle all the way.

Please don't misunderstand me. I am a Christian. I genuinely know the Lord as Savior and love Him. But when I heard the word *cancer*, it put the rubber of my faith right up against the road of reality. When I lay there in that hospital the first Monday night after Dr. Weston told me I had cancer, that's when the battle began. I wrestled with the Lord that night, just like Jacob in the Old Testament. During those dark hours, my mind went over and over the basic questions: *Am I really saved? Do I really know You, Lord?* For four or five hours I lay there in that bed in the dark before the Lord finally gave me a real peace.

That was the only time during that whole ordeal that I ever questioned the Lord about my personal salvation. I'm so grateful that He gave me peace in answer to that question.

Beyond that question, I did some deep soul searching, not unusual when thinking about the possibility of dying. But it was certainly out of the ordinary for someone my age to face death.

There are benefits to such an experience. As I lay there time after time in different hospitals, going through different procedures, I examined the basic questions: Is Christianity real? Is God alive? Through it all I've come to a stronger faith, and I've learned some valuable lessons in the process. In fact, there are four main lessons God taught me through this process that have convinced me of the reality of His presence and my faith in Him.

The first of those four is *His power to change lives*. When I look at people I've known who have had terrible lifestyles, mired in the pit of sin, and see how the Lord has changed their lives and given them a new hope, I have to say, "That's encouraging." I've read in the Scriptures of the many lives the Lord has changed, but when He transforms the lives of people you know personally, you realize there's nothing that can accomplish such an alteration but the power of God.

In our church congregation in Pennsylvania, I know of two men whose lives have been radically transformed. Morris Oberlin was an alcoholic before he came to Christ, and Bill Eck traveled the country playing guitar for various rock groups and was a heavy drug user. Today both of these men give strong testimonies of how God changed their lives completely. My experience with cancer has solidified my personal conviction of the Lord's power to change anyone.

The second factor God used to strengthen my faith was *creation*. I love the outdoors. I've spent a lot of time hunting, fishing, jogging and climbing. I remember one day in particular driving through an area in the Pocono Mountains to visit a customer of our company. It was about midway through my battle with cancer, during one of the times when I was feeling better. I looked around at this breathtaking beauty and thought, *Lord, this couldn't have just happened.*

In November 1994 we returned to Montana on another elk hunt, just like the one we took before I was diagnosed with cancer. This time I didn't get an elk, but I came away with something much more valuable— a vivid reminder of the reality and power of our awesome Creator God. This trip was especially meaningful because Dad had promised, "Chris, if you survive this transplant, I'll take you back to Montana on another hunting trip!" Just like our Heavenly Father, he came through on his promise.

The third thing God used to bolster my faith was the *truth of His Word.* So many times I was forced to look into His Word for promises, and God strengthened my faith as I meditated on those promises. I would think of those verses in Psalm 20, "May the Lord answer you when you are in distress; may the name of the God of Jacob protect you. May he send you help from the sanctuary and grant you support from Zion. . . . May he give you the desire of your heart and make all your plans succeed" (vv. 1-2, 4). Then there was the promise Tammy and Mary Beth mentioned, Proverbs 3:5-8: "Trust in the Lord with all your heart, and lean not on your own understanding; in all your ways acknowledge him, and he will make your paths straight. Do not be wise in your own eyes; fear the Lord and shun evil. This will bring health to your body and [marrow] to your bones." I saw that promise literally fulfilled!

There were so many Scripture verses God used to encourage and strengthen me. You may recall how my friend Dominique Herbst felt the Spirit prompting him to visit me in the hospital at what was probably my lowest point emotionally. At the celebration dinner a year after my transplant, Dominique told those who gathered about how God had impressed Romans 8:26 on his heart. It reads, "We do not know what we ought to pray for, but the Spirit himself intercedes for us with groans that words cannot express." Every time I think about how the Lord used Dominique in that situation, I get goose bumps!

On another occasion I was thinking through the last verses of 1 Corinthians 15, "Where, O death, is your victory? Where, O death, is your sting?" (v. 55). And, of course, Isaiah 40:31: "Those who hope in the Lord will renew their strength. They will soar on wings like eagles; they will run and not grow weary, they will walk and not be faint." Then there's 2 Corinthians 1:3-4, where Paul talks about God comforting us in all our troubles so we can comfort others who are in any trouble with the same comfort with which He has comforted us. I'm thankful for the many opportunities I've had to do that.

Before all this happened, I thought I had a strong commitment to God's Word, but it was nothing like my commitment to it and hunger for it now.

The fourth lesson the Lord taught me is how I have come to grips with *His sovereign control.* At times as I have told my story I have used the word *coincidence.* But as I told my pastor over the telephone one day when he called me in Arkansas, "As I look back on all that's happened, as far as I'm concerned you can take the word *coincidence* out of the dictionary. If you're a Christian, there's no such thing as coincidence." So many of the events I have related in this book have proven the validity of that statement.

The summer before I was diagnosed with cancer, my friend Tom Becker and I were standing in the hallway at church. Now Tom is one of those guys with whom I always talk about spiritual matters. On this particular occasion we were discussing where we were on our spiritual journey. I told Tom, "You know what I really need and what I'm going to start praying for is a greater compassion for people, especially for lost souls." At that point I began to pray for that.

Be careful what you ask God for. At the time I began praying that way, I had no idea what the Lord would allow me to go through to give me compassion!

But it wasn't the ordeal I went through that taught me as much as the care and concern of my church. Their prayers, their cards, their love to me are beyond measure. The Lord has used my church family to teach me what true love is. Many of them— people who have far less than we have— have given freely to us. Time and time again Heidi and I have sat and cried as we talked about their love and compassion.

Earlier I mentioned how Scott and Cathy Shaffer took in our two oldest daughters and supervised their school assignments while we were in Arkansas. Cathy is particularly gifted at seeing and responding to a need, such as washing dishes or ironing—whatever it took to assist Heidi during the months she struggled to be available to me in my many appointments and still care for the home and the girls.

My mother's cousin Dawn Hummel and her family also met many needs and gave significant support to Mary Beth when she was caring for our girls. During that time Dawn came in every Thursday to launder sheets and baby-sit so Mary Beth could have a little relief from her responsibility in caring for our daughters.

I really didn't fathom what Christlike love was until I experienced it firsthand. I witnessed people putting my needs and the needs of my family ahead of their own. God used individual after individual to convict me of my lack of Christlike compassion for others.

As I reflected on my response to people in need, I realized that these servants put me to shame. Before my cancer, when I would visit or call someone who was going through a trial, I would offer those hollow words, "Call me if you need anything." Though it made me feel better to fulfill my Christian "obligation," I realize now how insignificant those words really are.

Those words weren't good enough for the servants God sent to help me. They didn't wait for me to call; they called me. Not only did they call, they creatively found ways to serve our family. From sending us menus to fill out for meals, to mowing my grass and cleaning our home, they would not be denied the opportunity to show their love. What a lesson in Christlike servanthood!

I was the youth director at our church and also taught one of our young adult Sunday school classes. I enjoyed being a leader and teaching young people God's Word. There is no talk or lesson I could give, however, that would come close to having the impact these servants of

God had through their selfless giving.

I'm now convinced that, while serving in the trenches isn't very glamorous, it's far more effective than any other weapon the church has. Most of us admire the out-front, take-charge people who get most of the recognition. But I believe God's favor is toward those who serve behind the scenes out of love rather than for recognition.

We saw both the church family's compassion and God's providential care in what we came to call the "miracle yard sale." When my sister Tammy began to add up the expenses we had incurred because of plane fares and lodging during our many visits to Arkansas, she mentioned the idea of a yard sale to Scott Shaffer, who took it up with my Sunday school class. It was immediately adopted as a class project and was carried out without Heidi and me learning about it in advance.

They needed a location, so they selected a vacant lot along a heavily traveled commercial highway. The lot was in a great location, but it was covered with tall grass, and the owner insisted that they would have to obtain liability insurance.

Incredibly, God prompted the owner to make the lot available at no cost, then led someone else—we still have no idea who; it may have been a couple of angels for all we know—to cut the grass that covered the 20-plus acres. In fact, just before the sale, Scott drove past the lot and saw two huge mowers cutting the grass. When he returned to the office, he told the staff, "God's down there mowing the lot!"

There was no lack of goods to be sold. Household items, clothing and crafts were brought to the gym at our church, and it took an enclosed tractor-trailer van to deliver the goods to the site on the morning of the sale. What an incredible amount of love and concern was poured into this project on our behalf!

They also needed tents, food, and gas grills. God saw to it that all those items were donated, even "porta-potties." Through that yard sale more than $5,000 was raised toward our medical and travel expenses. We were overwhelmed the Sunday during the class session when we were presented with the proceeds.

God especially used this time to draw Heidi and me close to each other as well as closer to the Lord. During those difficult days, we frequently found ourselves talking about spiritual things, sharing valuable lessons about His presence.

Heidi told me there were two important truths God had impressed on her heart the day she found out I was diagnosed with cancer. The first is that God doesn't ask us to be successful. He doesn't call on us to fix everything that's wrong in our lives. He only wants us to be faithful with what we've been given. Second, Heidi felt a strong urgency— and I share that urgency— to show the world that we serve the same God when our life is falling apart that we do when everything seems to be going our way. As Heidi wrote during our time of recollection:

> *This was the beginning of a deep spiritual walk for me— a walk that I had never before experienced or knew could exist. The more I read about multiple myeloma, the more depressing it became. There was no known cure. I was not to get much encouragement from the medical field. None of my friends or family could give me any assurance that everything was going to be okay.*
>
> *I learned that in the day of adversity there is only one place to turn— that is to God. It was from this point that I began to make God's Word my major source of direction and comfort. Whenever I would feel afraid or confused and needed direction, I would go to my Bible.*
>
> *One of the first experiences I had with God speaking to me through His Word was on the same day we saw the doves. As I sat in church that morning, my mind wandered to the doves, and I felt prompted to see what the Bible had to say about doves. My concordance led me to the middle of Isaiah 38, and I went back to the beginning of the chapter to see what it was about. It was the story of King Hezekiah. Isaiah said that Hezekiah should get his house in order because he was going to die.*

The chapter tells how King Hezekiah pleaded with God to spare his life. God's response was to add 15 years to his life! The whole chapter was so very applicable to our situation! This was probably one of the first times God specifically used His Word to give me hope in our situation. At the time, I wasn't sure if this was God's voice or me reading what I wanted to hear. But as the months went on, different instances like this happened. God was beginning to teach me to discern His voice.

That brings me to another significant way in which God provided for me. He brought someone who was practically a stranger into my life to disciple me in learning to discern God's voice. She was following God's prompting to get involved in my life, while God was preparing me to let her into my life. Her name was Kathy Hackenberg, and as she reached out to me, God drew us together. This did not happen overnight; it occurred very slowly over about one-and-a-half years. All I can say is that due to Kathy's close walk with the Lord, He would prompt her to call or write to me time after time, at exactly those points when I felt the depths of despair.

I especially recall one time when she called. We were at a point where there seemed such little hope. I had so much to do with caring for the children and helping them with their homework, preparing meals, etc., that I didn't think I was going to make it. That night I received a call from her, wondering if I was doing okay. I proceeded to tell her what a difficult time I was going through. Kathy responded by reminding me to rest and do my tasks. She felt God had called her to intercede for me. I was to rest, and she would carry the burden for me for a while. I felt remarkable peace and relief.

About three months after Chris's transplant, Kathy and I began to get together periodically. Before long, our hearts were united. I know that God had sent her into my life to uphold me and teach me to discern God's voice as I walked this dark and

*lonely path. I will be forever grateful to God for send-
ing her into my life.*

Not only did Heidi and I draw closer during this time, but we both began to see additional evidences of God's presence, protection and provision. Let me mention three specific incidents that demonstrate how God answered.

The first of these occurred in May 1992 following my diagnosis. I was wrestling with questions about whether God really existed, as well as just trying to find some hope. I began praying like never before that somehow God would give me some encouragement— particularly encouragement about my physical condition, and that I might be able to beat this disease.

One Thursday morning in May as I was working in my office, sorting the mail in my tray, I found a card from someone named Sharon Barber. Since that name was not familiar, I opened the card right away. She told me that she had read about my diagnosis with multiple myeloma in the prayer request column of LifeAction Ministries' magazine.

She went on to express her concern and her prayer support for me. Then she said she also wanted to encourage me and let me know that her closest friend had been diagnosed with myeloma and had just celebrated her seventh year of being cancer-free since her bone marrow transplant!

That was just the encouragement I needed! I immediately went into the bathroom at our office and began to cry like a baby. I wept for two reasons. First, I was overjoyed to know that someone else had walked this journey and was alive after seven years. There really was hope! Second, I was so grateful that God had heard my cries for encouragement. I remember telling Him that morning in the bathroom, "Lord, my faith is so weak, forgive me. But please walk with me, and when I hit my lowest, Lord, just help me, let me know You are there."

A second incident occurred prior to my first transplant. I needed to get some information and statistics together from the Arkansas Cancer Research Center in order to write a letter to our insurance company to try to persuade them to pay for the transplant. As I gathered this information, I again felt overwhelmed by all the statistics concerning multiple myeloma. As I read the prognosis for this disease and scanned the grim statistics, I again became very discouraged.

A sense of depression persisted for several days, but I never told anyone how I felt, including Heidi. About the third day of this depressed state, when I returned home from work, Heidi said I was supposed to call Clair Berge. Clair is a good friend and a deacon in our church. He's always had a special burden for our family and had really showed a lot of concern.

When I phoned Clair, he started by apologizing for not calling me earlier, but he said something had happened to him and he felt he needed to tell me about it. He explained that the previous night he began dreaming and thinking about me. Finally, he couldn't sleep any longer, so he got up, went downstairs and began to pray specifically for me.

He said never before did he have such a burden to pray for someone. After pouring out his heart, asking the Lord to deliver me, he felt led to open his Bible and read some Scripture. The first verse he read was John 11:4. This passage about Lazarus states, "This sickness will not end in death. No, it is for God's glory so that God's Son may be glorified through it."

Clair said, "Chris, you know me. I am not a person who looks for signs and wonders. I've never experienced anything like this in my life before, but the Lord spoke to me concerning this verse and you. I haven't told anyone about it except Deb. But the Lord wouldn't give me any peace until I called you."

Deb, his wife, is our receptionist at the office. The next day as I discussed this experience with her, she confirmed that she had never seen Clair the way he was that morning when he told her what had happened. I believed this was a personal message God sent through one of His servants to keep me encouraged.

A third incident came as I was collecting and sorting through my experiences in preparation for this book. One of my closest friends, Barry Goodling, called me. He and I attended high school together, roomed together in college and played soccer in both high school and college. He is now vice president of development at Messiah College. More importantl, he is a dear brother in Christ.

Over the past two years, he and his wife have been put to the test. Their son, who is now four, was diagnosed with Wilms' tumor, a form of kidney cancer. Although the original prognosis was encouraging, he has since had several relapses and was scheduled for a third surgery when Barry called. His prognosis is not good.

As I spoke with Barry on the phone, we reflected on these past months of chemotherapy, surgery and bad test results. Then he said, "You know, Chris, it seems whenever we reach our lowest points, when we feel we can't go on or we cry out, 'God, are You really there?' that somehow, some way, God always evidences Himself."

After my experiences I couldn't agree more. Whenever I would cry out, or even felt too low to try, at my most desperate moments God always sent someone or something to let me know His presence was with me. In turn, I hope I can be an encouragement to others who may be walking this difficult path.

I couldn't end this chapter without discussing the compassion of my family. They stood together with me in such an incredible fashion. Back in May 1993, when we were staying at the Guest House in Little Rock, our pastor wrote me a letter in which he described how he had seen God working in my life, primarily in a spiritual way rather than a physical one. He commented on the providential direction God had given and how our Lord had given both specific tokens of His presence and biblical promises.

Then he said something in the letter that was so encouraging I want to quote it to you:

I stand in awe of your family from a spiritual standpoint. I honor your father as one of the pre-eminent Christians I've ever known. I think of something that happened years ago in New England. During a class at Yale, a student asked a professor to define a Christian. The professor reflected for a few moments as he looked out the window at the sprawling campus, then he rose and pointed out the window and said, "There goes one." He was pointing to the saintly Phillips Brooks, who was walking along the sidewalk.

If I would define a Christian in human terms, I would say, "Look at Max Bingaman—there is a Christian." Chris, if you keep going the way you are going now, I'll be able to say the same thing about you.

I deeply appreciate Pastor John Thornbury and his wife, Reta. I'm especially grateful for the way John described the Christian commitment of my dad and, for that matter, my entire family. We were all in this together.

Speaking of my dad, one incident involving him is etched in my memory. During the time when I had a collapsed vertebra, I experienced numerous periods of severe pain. At times, the only way I could find relief was to lie flat on the floor with my face down. One Saturday morning one of those spells came over me, and I was lying face down in the family room in terrible pain, just trying to get some relief. I heard a car drive up. The car door opened and I was sure by the time of morning it was and by the sound of footsteps that it was my dad.

As he entered the room, Dad saw me on the floor. He had seen me in that position before and knew what was going on. He came over and knelt down with me as I lay there on the floor. All he said was, "Oh, son." As I lay there face down, I felt his hot tears falling on my cheek. Then he began to pray. "Oh, God," he cried out. "You know I've prayed and asked You to remove the pain from this boy. My prayer is, Lord, if You'll just take this pain from him. Or, Lord, let me bear the pain for him."

I knew before then that my dad loved me, but never before had I felt the strength of a father's love for a son the way I felt it that morning.

Later as I began to feel some relief from the pain, I remembered another Father who watched His Son suffer.

He could have taken that pain away. His Son even prayed, "Father, let this cup pass from Me."

Yet the Father saw fit to allow Jesus to suffer and die because of His love for you and me. I can't comprehend that kind of love, but I'm so thankful for what God did in sending His Son to die on the cross for our sins.

You see, even if I never have another cancer cell in my body, I still will die someday unless the Lord returns first. I have had to face the reality of death in a way few people do who survive, and I am thankful for that. In fact, I have told a lot of people, "You really aren't ready to live until you're ready to die." And now that I have faced death, I can say with conviction that I am more thankful than ever for the eternal hope we have in Jesus Christ.

The Lord used my time in the hospitals, especially in Arkansas, to open my heart to care about people who need the Lord. I have worked, lived and worshiped mostly with Christians or at least people with moral convictions. We have a Christian family. We spend a lot of time involved at church. So it would be accurate to say I have lived in a "sheltered" area of the world.

But the Lord pulled me right out of that world and put me in a cancer clinic in Arkansas where people from all walks of life were facing death. As I began talking with those people, whenever there were times I even hinted about being a Christian or said anything spiritual, I was shocked at how they would react. There were several who said, "Don't you shake your finger at me and tell me what I'm doing wrong. Don't give me that Christianity bit."

Hearing them say things like that blew me away. I didn't know what they were talking about or why they were reacting that way at the time. But the longer I listened, the more I learned. I began realizing that often all we do as Christians is shake our finger at lost people. Often we spend more time telling them what they are doing wrong than listening to their problems and hurts and caring about them the way the Jesus did. We often respond to sinners more like the Pharisees did. Sometimes we are just like one person put it, "A finger-pointing, tongue-lashing group of hypocrites."

Now, I'm not saying this to condemn other Christians; I just know the Lord used those things to convict me. I sat in church in Pennsylvania one Sunday morning, worshiping and thinking, *Here we are, you sinners. Come get our Gospel and get saved.* I believe it was Chuck Swindoll who said, "People don't care how much you know until they know how much you care."

When I came home after the transplant, Pastor Thornbury asked me if my theology had changed. "No," I told him. But then as I thought about it, I said, "I don't think my theology has changed, but I hope the way I apply it has. I want to show the kind of compassion to lost people that the church family has shown to me. I want to love people the way the Heavenly Father who sent His Son to die for them did. I want to hold out God's Word to people, not as a sword to cut them down or condemn them, but as a ray of hope to draw them to the eternal life He so graciously provided. John 3:17 says, "For God did not send his Son into the world to condemn the world, but to save the world through Him."

As I have told many people since my ordeal, "The Lord gave me a good gift, the gift of life for 34 years, a gift I didn't deserve. If He sees fit to give me some more time, I just want to use that time to serve Him."

My battle with cancer has in one sense been a monument to God's grace. It's like the stones of remembrance the Israelites set up after they came across the Jordan River. I don't think any of them wanted to go back through that ordeal in the wilderness, and I certainly don't want to go back through those three years again. But I never want to forget any of the lessons the Lord has taught me. In fact, if my vision begins to blur or my passion for serving Christ wavers, I want to look back and use this time in my life as a reminder of everything God has done for me. As Paul said in Romans 11:36, "For from him and through him and to him are all things. To him be the glory forever! Amen."

Chapter 15

The Source
of Real Hope

If there is one thing I would like to convey through this book, it's the importance of hope. I certainly have learned the role of hope in overcoming my cancer, and I think the hope for my recovery is being fulfilled. But that is not the most important hope of all. There is nothing more valuable than the eternal hope we can have in Jesus Christ. Talk about an anchor to hang on to during the storms of life! I have learned firsthand from staring death in the face that the only hope that matters is the hope we have in Jesus.

One of the things Don Hawkins and I talked about as we were preparing to write this book was the different ways people use the word *hope*. Most of them are quite different from the biblical meaning of the term. For example, I am a Penn State Nittany Lions fan. Cut my arm, and I bleed Nittany blue! Every fall when college football kicks off, I hope they will claim another national championship.

I also am hopeful that the lumber business will remain stable and even grow, that my parents and family will experience good health, that my girls will grow up and do well, and that Heidi and I will enjoy long and happy lives.

While it is certainly appropriate to hope for all those things, I would be a fool to say that any of them are certainties. The Bible describes hope in a different way, as something that is absolutely positive, a future certainty. Don describes it in his book *Never Give Up* as "a positive expectation regarding the future, based firmly on a fact from the past— the resurrection of Jesus Christ from the dead."

My ultimate hope for the future is not based on the best medical care, although I am certainly thankful for it. Nor is it based on the love of family and friends, though I am extremely grateful for that. In fact, my ultimate hope isn't even based on the bone marrow transplant I received from Mary Beth, though it clearly saved my life.

I am convinced the Bible is true when it says every one of us has been born with a spiritual cancer called sin. Just as cancer cells in a person's body can cause them to die, so it is spiritually with sin. The Bible makes it clear in Romans 3:23 that all of us have sinned and fallen short of God's glory and perfection. According to the apostle Paul, the consequence of sin is death— spiritual death, eternal separation from God.

The only way I could live was to receive a transplant— a transplant that would ultimately remove all the cancer cells from my body.

When I was lying on a hospital gurney on the transplant floor, my sister willingly boarded an elevator and went down seven floors below me. There she underwent an operation to give me her healthy bone marrow.

Before that happened, the doctors had given me such a strong dose of chemotherapy that, as they explained it, I was doomed to die if I didn't receive the bone marrow transplant.

As I lay there on that bed, they brought those two bags in and said, "Here's your bone marrow." Those two bags held my only hope to keep living!

My sister had given her marrow for me. I was dying and needed it. Those bags were hung on a pole so they could drain into my body; otherwise, they wouldn't have done me one bit of good. I thank God that, as I received that bone marrow into my body, it cleansed me from cancer.

Recently I read another story about how a substitutionary death helped others beat cancer. Stacy McKay, a 23-year-old graduate of Purdue University, didn't survive her bone marrow transplant. After the operation she seemed to progress well, but 75 days after her transplant she died of aspergillosis. The same intensive therapy that killed her healthy blood cells that had been infected by cancer weakened her immune system and put her at risk of the infection that ultimately took her life.

According to officials of the National Bone Marrow Donor Program, however, Stacy and her family and friends were responsible for adding nearly 5,000 people who heard about her plight to the National Bone Marrow Registry, and more than $75,000 was raised in her name to subsidize donor registry programs.

I have encouraged the men and women at our company to consider registering for a bone marrow transplant. It's a wonderful way to demonstrate the love of Christ, to make yourself available for someone else who may need what you have. Best of all, the process of a bone marrow transplant clearly illustrates that sacrificial act of Jesus, who shed His blood for us and rose again that we might benefit from the promise of His presence.

My experience has provided a vivid picture of what Christ has done for all of us. Just as Mary Beth gave her bone marrow for me, He shed His blood on the cross for us that we might be cleansed of the spiritual cancer of sin. Because of His death and resurrection we now have an eternal hope, one that is far greater than any hope we might cling to in this life. Through it we are empowered to face the problems and pain of life, including cancer.

I learned firsthand how frightening it is to walk into a doctor's office when you know he's going to give you test results, and whatever he says will have a drastic effect on your future. That's nerve-wracking! But how much worse would it be to stand before the Great Physician, have Him pull out the chart of what's happened in your life and say, "I'm sorry, you'll have to depart from Me. I never knew you. You never trusted My sacrifice for your sin."

That's why one of my ultimate goals is to use my experience to relate to everyone who reads this book the truth that you can have the promise of God's presence and the hope of eternal life by placing your trust in Him. It's very simple. Admit you're a sinner, affected by the malignancy of evil and unable to free yourself. Then place your trust in Jesus Christ, God's perfect Son, who died in your place on the cross and rose again from the dead. You can tell Him by praying a prayer something like this— the exact words are not the important thing; it's the trust in your heart that counts:

> *Lord Jesus, I admit I'm a sinner and cannot save myself. I turn from my sin to You, believing that as God's perfect Son You died on the cross for me and rose again. I trust You right now to forgive my sins and give me everlasting life. Thank You for saving me.*

If you place your trust in Him, then the promise of His presence is yours— for every situation you face in life, and for all eternity. I trust if you haven't made that decision to receive Him, you'll do so right now, even as you are reading. Just as in the case of cancer, delay can be deadly.

Date Due

5-10-98			
5-24			
6-21			
OCT 8 2000			

Code 4386-04, CLS-4, Broadman Supplies, Nashville, Tenn.,
Printed in U.S.A.